JUDE

The Acts of the Apostates

By

S. MAXWELL CODER

*The text of Jude quoted is the
American Standard Version of 1901*

MOODY PRESS • CHICAGO

CONTENTS

Copyright ©, 1958 by
THE MOODY BIBLE INSTITUTE
OF CHICAGO

ISBN: 0-8024-2065-6

STRANGE AND TERRIBLE WORDS

THE BEGINNING OF THE AGE of the Church is described in the Acts of the Apostles. The end of the Church Age is set forth in the Epistle of Jude, which might well be called the Acts of the Apostates. The first book which can properly be said to contain Church history describes the deeds and teachings of men of God through whom Christ began to build His Church. The last epistle of the New Testament relates the deeds and teaching of evil men who will be living upon the earth as the history of the professing Church comes to an end.

Jude is the only book in all God's Word entirely devoted to the great apostasy which is to come upon Christendom before the Lord Jesus Christ returns. This brief message of twenty-five verses is the vestibule to the Revelation, introducing the Bible student to the apocalyptic judgments unfolded therein.

Without Jude, the prophetic picture which begins with the teachings of Christ in the Gospels and develops throughout the epistles would be incomplete. Our Lord raised the question: "When the Son of man cometh, shall he find faith on the earth?" (Luke 18:8). Paul supplied us with the terminology commonly used by Bible students concerning a falling away from the faith of our fathers in the last days. He called it "the apostasy" (II Thess. 2:3, marg.). He described it as a departure from the faith (I Tim. 4:1), an unwillingness to endure sound doctrine (II Tim. 4:3). Through the apostle Peter, the Holy Spirit revealed that false teachers would some day appear and bring in "damnable

3

heresies, even denying the Lord that bought them" (II Peter 2:1; 3:3).

Jude brings the teaching of the entire Bible about apostasy to a tremendous climax. He takes us back to the very dawn of human history. We are reminded of apostasy at the gate of Eden and within God's ancient people Israel. Our thoughts are turned to princes and prophets, to saints and sinners, to eternal fire and everlasting darkness, to the sea and to the stars, to past judgments and future glory. We are taken into the unseen world for a strange and terrible story of the sin of fallen angels, and another story of a dispute between Michael the archangel and Satan, those antagonists who are set over against each other once more in mortal combat in Revelation 12.

It is a remarkable fact that the Epistle of Jude has suffered neglect by Bible students and preachers in spite of its wealth of revelation and the tremendous sweep of its subject matter. The great expositor Alexander Maclaren, whose works have been published in seventeen volumes, has given us only three sermons on it. The twenty-five volumes of Biblical studies by Joseph Parker, known as *The People's Bible,* contain but a single message on Jude. Only five pages in six thick books are devoted to this epistle in the beloved Jamieson, Fausset, and Brown *Critical and Experimental Commentary.* Of 844 pages in the great *Bible Commentary* dealing with Hebrews through Revelation a mere fourteen were set aside for this final epistle of the New Testament. There are twenty-three pages on Jude in the monumental *Lange's Commentary* of twenty-five large volumes.

Why should such a rich storehouse of Bible truth have been so seriously neglected? The answer may lie in the fact that Jude deals largely with conditions in the last days. The rising of the present high tide of apostasy within the professing Church has been necessary to call attention to the import of the epistle as a whole. Jude must no longer be considered a mysterious book, offering only two or three verses of value in the ministry of the Word of God.

The possibility that the denial of our holy faith, so widespread in our own generation, may be a prelude to the great apostasy referred to by our Lord (Luke 18:8) should quicken our interest in this final epistle during these momentous times. If the last page of history of the Church is about to be turned, we may expect the Holy Spirit to give us new light on the strange and terrible words and warnings of Jude. A fresh study may awaken us to a solemn realization that it is later than we think, so that we shall pray and work as never before, with the confident expectation of revival within the Body of Christ and an ingathering of many souls before the great and terrible day of the Lord shall come.

Bible students have wrestled with the problem of outlining the Epistle of Jude or indicating its main divisions. Even though a completely satisfactory outline may be difficult to prepare (largely because of the richness of the contents), a careful study of the internal structure of the epistle reveals a mathematical progression of truth which clearly shows the hand of God in its design. No one would think that the one who wrote this short letter was following any particular pattern, and yet there is something in the way these great truths have been put together which reminds us of basic laws underlying the structure of the universe itself—the universe which came from the same creative hand that has given us the Bible.

Jude begins with a salutation containing a threefold blessing; it ends with a doxology containing a statement of the threefold heritage of the Lord's people. Salvation is mentioned in the third verse from the beginning and in the third verse from the end. We are exhorted to contend for the faith in verse 3, and to build ourselves up on our faith in verse 20. "Remember the Old Testament" is the theme of verse 5; "remember the New Testament" is the theme of verse 17. Such parallels of truth are easily discovered as we move toward the heart of the epistle. Some of them may be seen in the accompanying structural outline.

A structural outline of Jude

Assurance for the Christian (vv. 1, 2)
 The believer and the faith (v. 3)
  Apostates described (v. 4)
   Apostasy in Old Testament history (vv. 5-8)
    Apostasy in the supernatural realm (vv. 9, 10)
     An ancient trio of apostates (v. 11)
    Apostasy in the natural realm (vv. 12, 13)
   Apostasy in Old Testament prophecy (vv. 14-16)
  Apostates described (vv. 17-19)
 The believer and the faith (vv. 20-23)
Assurance for the Christian (vv. 24, 25)

COMFORT FOR CHRISTIANS

Jude, a servant of Jesus Christ, and brother of James, to them that are called, beloved in God the Father, and kept for Jesus Christ" (v.1).

THE FIRST WORD of this epistle is the signature of the man through whom the Holy Spirit gave His message to the Church. Like Paul in his epistles, Jude placed his name at the very beginning.

In the original Greek, this name is Judas. On the very threshold of a book written about apostasy appears a name which brings to mind a traitor who stands forever as the worst apostate the world has ever known. Judas, a name common enough in the days of our Lord, has been anathema for nearly two thousand years. Men call their sons Paul or Peter, they call their dogs Nero or Caesar, but the name *Judas* has been blotted out of our language except as a synonym of apostasy and treachery.

Nevertheless, God was pleased to choose a man bearing this name as the writer of the treatise on apostasy which we are privileged to study. There is certainly an important reason for such a choice. What better title could be found in human language for this epistle which sets forth the falling away within the professing Church of the last days? In the providence of God the one word *Judas* has been written in large letters over this inspired description of what it means when men turn away from the truth of the Word of God.

Before identifying himself in earthly relationships, Jude sets forth his heavenly relationship. He was "a servant of

Jesus Christ," which means literally he was Christ's bondslave. Here is supplied the true key to the understanding of
an amazing book. Unless we too put our blessed Lord first,
making Him absolute Lord of our lives, we shall find little
profit in the study of this epistle of a man who did give
Christ the pre-eminence. Unless we count ourselves also
bondslaves of Jesus Christ, much of the Word of God will
be obscure and uninteresting to us. It is a striking fact that
the Book of Revelation, to which Jude introduces us, begins
with a statement that God gave it to Jesus Christ "to show
unto his servants." That is, only the bondslaves of Jesus
Christ are given the privilege of understanding these prophetic pages at the end of the Bible.

Jude was "brother of James," who was head of the church
at Jerusalem, and author of the Epistle of James. James is
called "the Lord's brother" in Galatians 1:19. This means
that Jude was one of the four brothers of the Lord Jesus
mentioned in Mark 6:3, who grew up with Him in Nazareth.
Our Lord spoke of these children in the home of Mary as
"my brethren . . . my mother's children" (Ps. 69:7, 8).

With becoming humility—or perhaps because they did not
believe on Him at one time (John 7:5)—neither of these
brothers mentions his human relationship to the Lord Jesus.
Neither James nor Jude was numbered among the twelve
apostles. The books these brothers wrote present one simi-
larity in content. James sets forth good works as real evidence of saving faith; Jude sets forth evil works as real evidence of apostasy.

Those for whom this epistle is intended are called, beloved, and kept. The Trinity is involved in our salvation.
Our calling is the work of the Holy Spirit; we are beloved in
the Father; we are kept for Jesus Christ. This threefold
declaration presents a most astonishing and comforting series
of truths for the encouragement of all God's people in days
of darkness, delusion and doctrines of demons within the
professing Church.

Before we plunge into the terrible contents of Jude, there

to read of the judgment and eternal vengeance of God upon all who turn away from the truth of His Word, we are comforted and encouraged with some of the sweetest words of assurance to be found anywhere in the Bible. Lest we might fear that the apostasy and false teaching of the last days may sweep us away, God assures our hearts that He has called us, that He loves us, and that He is keeping us for His Son, no matter what happens around us.

Who are the called? The Scriptures reply: "God hath from the beginning chosen you to salvation through sanctification of the Spirit and belief of the truth: whereunto he called you by our gospel, to the obtaining of the glory of our Lord Jesus Christ" (II Thess. 2:13, 14).

Those who are called are those who, hearing the Gospel, have been so deeply convicted by the Holy Spirit that they have believed the truth and received the Saviour who died for their sins and rose again from the dead. They have been brought "out of darkness into his marvelous light" (I Peter 2:9). The Saviour issued the call, "Come unto me." Jude addresses his epistle to all who have heard this call and responded.

In Romans 8:28-30, the fact of our calling is central in five statements having to do with our salvation. God foreknew, predestinated, called, justified, and glorified us. He has been pleased to write all of these things in the past tense. Our glorification is as certain as our calling and our justification.

Who are the "beloved in God the Father"? The Lord Jesus has given us the answer in John 17:20, 23. They are those whom God has loved as He loves His own Son. They are all who have believed on the Son of God through the word of His ambassadors. Our Saviour said: "The Father himself loveth you, because ye have loved me, and have believed that I came out from God" (John 16:27). He said again: "If a man love me, he will keep my words: and my Father will love him, and we will come unto him, and make our abode with him" (John 14:23).

That we are to be "kept for Jesus Christ" is an exceedingly precious and heartwarming truth. A minister of my acquaintance still looks back, after many years, to his discovery of this fact. While on vacation one summer, he was reading the New Testament in the American Standard Version, and came to the Book of Jude. When he noted the words "kept for Jesus Christ," he sat up in astonishment, read the words over again, and then reveled in the wonder of what was to him one of the greatest discoveries of his life. Never before had he noticed the phrase, which is translated differently in the King James Version.

The word *kept* in the original expresses watchful care, or close attention, and is suggestive of present possession. It is used of Peter's and Paul's imprisonments in Acts 12:5 and 25:4, 21. It is also used in I Peter 1:4 of our inheritance reserved in Heaven for us.

There is an illuminating detail in this passage which has not been brought over into the English translations. The original language uses the perfect tense, of which the nearest equivalent is "continually kept." It is a continuing result of a past action; it looks all the way to the coming of Jesus Christ for His own.

A comparison between Jude and other New Testament letters reveals that this word *kept* does not appear in the salutation of any other epistle. Paul refers to his readers as "beloved" and "called," but Jude adds the word *kept*. Is it because the keeping work of God will be sorely needed by those who live in the last evil days of the great apostasy? A forward look to the return of Christ, for whom we are kept by the power of God (I Peter 1:5), will encourage every true believer. Jude supplies us with the inspired answer to the prayer of Christ: "Holy Father, keep through thine own name those whom thou hast given me" (John 17:11).

An instructive word study is to be found here. Although we are kept continually, according to verse 1, we are nevertheless to keep ourselves in the love of God (v. 21). There is a Godward side to this blessed truth, and a manward side as well. By way of contrast, the fallen angels in verse 6 are said to be kept continually awaiting judgment, for the reason that they kept not their first estate.

Thank God for all that is involved in this blessed doctrine of the safekeeping of the believer! No matter how terrible the apostasy which may settle down upon the professing Church, nor how sore the afflictions through which we must pass, we are kept for Jesus Christ. While we are being kept, we are beloved of God the Father as His called and chosen ones. As we keep the Word of His patience, He will keep us from the hour of tribulation which shall come upon all the world (Rev. 3:10). By obeying the exhortation to keep ourselves in the love of God, it is possible for our whole spirit and soul and body to be kept blameless unto the coming of our Lord Jesus Christ (I Thess. 5:23).

He is able even to guard us from stumbling until that day finally dawns. After it has come, we will know far more of the wonder of the power of God which guarantees our safekeeping and makes our heavenly inheritance sure; but for the time being, it is sufficient for us to rest in these blessed truths simply on the authority of His Word.

MERCY MULTIPLIED

Mercy unto you and peace and love be multiplied (v. 2).

THE SALUTATION of Jude is far more than a courteous expression at the beginning of a letter. Like other Scripture, it is given by inspiration of God, and is profitable (II Tim. 3:16). It is important for doctrine, for reproof, for correction, for instruction in righteousness. Neglected though it has been, it is the only such statement in the entire Bible.

We know that there is a divine order in the familiar salutation of Paul, "grace to you, and peace," for grace must always precede peace. There is likewise a divine order in the multiplication of mercy, peace, and love in Jude 2.

This epistle has to do with apostasy in the last time (v. 18). God's people will need mercy in those days. Mercy is divine pity expressing itself in help for the needy. It presupposes need and helplessness.

The word *mercy* stands over the threshold of this epistle of the apostasy, introducing a somber picture. Where the word *law* is over a door, we find death (Num. 15:32-36) and failure (James 2:10), with Christ the only remedy (Gal. 3:24). The door designated *works* leads us to a chamber of horrors (Gal. 5:19-21). Grace opens upon the riches of undeserved favor. God, who is rich in mercy (Eph. 2:4), exhorts us in His Word to "come boldly to the throne of grace, that we may obtain mercy, and find grace to help in time of need" (Heb. 4:16). Such a time will surely come.

Peace is the second great Bible word to be multiplied for believers in the last days. There is no peace for the wicked

12

(Isa. 57:20, 21), but "we have peace with God through our Lord Jesus Christ" (Rom. 5:1). Already this is the portion of those to whom Jude writes, but they will need more of the peace of God, which passeth all understanding. As D. L. Moody wrote in the margin of his Bible at Philippians 4:6, 7: "This is ours when we worry about nothing, pray about everything, thank God for anything." It is to garrison our hearts until the Lord comes and takes us to our eternal peace.

The third word in our verse is *love,* the bond uniting believers to their Lord and to one another. It is the first commandment of Christ: "A new commandment I give unto you, that ye love one another. . . . By this shall all men know that ye are my disciples" (John 13:34, 35).

In one form or another the word *love* appears in each of the first three verses of Jude. It must be important. It may suggest that an outstanding reason for apostasy is lack of love among brethren. Philadelphia is followed by Laodicea. When love is absent, men outside the true Church lack evidence that we are indeed disciples of Christ.

Here are the mercy of God, the peace of God, the love of God. They reappear at the close of the epistle, bringing into focus the holy Trinity once more. We are to keep ourselves in the love of God the Father (v. 21), to look for the mercy of our Lord Jesus Christ unto eternal life (v. 21), to keep praying in the Holy Spirit (v. 20), the key to the experience of the peace of God (Phil. 4:6, 7).

There is an upward look in the word *mercy,* an inward look in the word *peace,* an outward look in the word *love.* These three relate us properly to God, to our own inner being, to our brethren around us. When they are multiplied, and only then, will we be able to cope with the great apostasy of the last days.

COMPELLED TO WRITE

Beloved, while I was giving all diligence to write unto you of our common salvation, I was constrained to write unto you exhorting you to contend earnestly for the faith which was once for all delivered unto the saints (v. 3).

THE MESSAGE OF JUDE is addressed to the beloved of the Lord. God's Word is for God's people. It will have little meaning to those who have not been born into His family, for "the natural man receiveth not the things of the Spirit of God: for they are foolishness unto him: neither can he know them, because they are spiritually discerned" (I Cor. 2:14).

How wonderful that we are the beloved of the Lord! There are two words for *love* in the original Greek of the New Testament. One of them, *phileo,* stands for human or family love. It is so used in Matthew 10:37. Although it may be fervent and enduring, it also may be fickle and changing.

The other, higher word for love, *agapao,* is the one used in Jude. It is the word for divine love, never changing. It is the love of John 3:16, the love which is shed abroad in our hearts by the Holy Spirit. How much it means to be the recipients of this kind of love, especially when called to pass through suffering!

"Beloved," said the Lord through Peter, "think it not strange concerning the fiery trial which is to try you, as though some strange thing happened unto you: but rejoice, inasmuch as ye are partakers of Christ's sufferings" (I Peter

14

4:12). Back of the love which led the apostles to write stands the eternal, changeless love of our God. Here is another encouragement for Christians in days of apostasy.

As Jude was diligently preparing to write about our common salvation, something happened which changed his mind. There came to him a definite compulsion to write about the defense of our most holy faith. What might otherwise have been merely a letter from one believer to another became a letter by the Holy Spirit to the whole Church, a part of the sacred canon of Scripture.

The "common salvation" to which he refers is the common property of all believers. It is necessary alike for the outcast who lives in open sin, and the virtuous welfare worker whose life is blameless in the sight of men. There is no respect of persons with God. Except a man be born again, he cannot see the kingdom of God.

The compulsion which Jude experienced may be rendered literally, "I had necessity." The same expression is found in Acts 17:3: "Christ *must needs* have suffered, and risen again from the dead." He must needs die for our sins; the Holy Spirit must needs warn us through Jude that men will deny the necessity for that death. Such denial must be resisted by the saints.

Paul wrote of a similar compulsion. "Necessity is laid upon me; yea, woe is unto me, if I preach not the gospel" (I Cor. 9:16). The overwhelming power of the Holy Spirit compelled him to preach.

The root meaning of this expression in the Greek is "to compress." Pressure was brought to bear upon Jude; therefore our epistle is not a human document, but a message from the hand of God. No doubt Jude's diligence commended him to the Lord; but his words are the choice of the Spirit Himself, to instruct His people concerning those who creep into the church, bringing with them damnable heresies.

It is important to realize that the Epistle of Jude is the result of the constraining, overwhelming wisdom and power of the Holy Spirit and that the message is expressed in the exact words God wants us to have. Thus Jude takes his

place with those of whom it is written: "The prophecy came
not in old time by the will of man: but holy men of God
spake as they were moved by the Holy Ghost" (II Peter
1:21).

The first God-breathed exhortation to come from Jude is
that we are to be contending earnestly for the faith once for
all delivered to the saints.

It is a striking fact that the Greek word *exhort* is the verb
of the noun *Paraclete,* applied to the Holy Spirit as our
Comforter in John 16:7. The *Paraclete* is "one called alongside to help." There is a sense in which, through this epistle,
Jude is called to our side to help us with counsel and ad-
vice in a time of great darkness.

What does it mean to contend earnestly for the faith? "To
contend earnestly" is but one word in the original, meaning
"to agonize upon." Even though our English word *agony*
may not have the exact connotation in our language as the
original from which it has been taken, it is clear that we
must take seriously the defense of our most holy faith.
Bagster's *Greek Lexicon* renders this word, "to contend
strenuously in defense of," a meaning which should be kept
clearly in mind.

Each believer who respects all of God's Word must decide
as in the presence of the Lord whether or not he is faithfully
following Jude's exhortation. We are contending for the
faith when we strengthen the hands of faithful pastors who
are honoring the Word of God in their pulpits. We are contending for the faith when we give an unflinching witness
for our blessed Saviour, when we distribute tracts, when we
make possible the training of faithful ambassadors for Christ,
when we withhold support and encouragement from those
who compromise or deny the whole counsel of God, when
we speak out against the preaching of another Gospel.

The Sunday school teacher who is true to the Scriptures
is contending for the faith as surely as the missionary who
lives in the midst of paganism. It is written: "Cease, my son,
to hear the instruction that causeth to err from the words of
knowledge" (Prov. 19:27). It is likewise written: "Be

watchful, and strengthen the things which remain, that are ready to die" (Rev. 3:2). Each man must be fully persuaded in his own mind, as before God, what he must do in any set of circumstances in obedience to Jude 3.

Light upon this subject is shed again by the structure of this epistle. In verse 3 we are required to contend for the faith, in verse 20 we are required to be building up ourselves on our most holy faith.

There is an Old Testament illustration of this twofold attitude of the believer toward the faith. When Nehemiah's men were building the wall of Jerusalem, enemies sought to keep them from it, just as enemies seek to keep us from carrying on God's work today. "Everyone with one of his hands wrought in the work, and with the other hand held a weapon. For the builders, everyone had his sword girded by his side, and so builded. And he that sounded the trumpet was by me" (Neh. 4:17, 18).

The parallel in Jude is remarkable. On the one hand, we are to be building ourselves up in the faith; on the other hand, we are to be contending earnestly for the faith. Nehemiah's men had swords of steel. We have the Sword of the Spirit, which is the Word of God. As we build for the Lord, we must defend ourselves against our great adversary and all who are deceived by him into denying our faith. Those who labored in Nehemiah's day were constantly alert for the sound of the trumpet. We are listening for the trump of God, which will end our struggle against all the powers of darkness.

Our contending is to be for "the faith." The Spirit of God did not use the word *salvation,* nor the word *Gospel.* The faith concerns our salvation, it has much to do with the Gospel, but it is a more inclusive term than either. The faith is that extensive body of Bible doctrine which makes up the perfect whole of the truth revealed by God concerning our common salvation.

Inasmuch as Christians are urged in II Corinthians 13:5: "Examine yourselves, whether ye be in the faith; prove your own selves," it is important that we understand just what the faith is. No one passage defines it. An examination of some eighteen occurrences of the expression is necessary to determine its meaning. Some of the elements may be briefly indicated.

The faith is a mystery (I Tim. 3:9), that is, something not revealed prior to New Testament times. It is that which will be departed from in the last days (I Tim. 4:1), and therefore includes the historic creedal position of Bible believers for nineteen hundred years. It involves duty to others (I Tim. 5:8). Faithful teaching of revealed truth establishes churches in the faith (Acts 16:5).

Therefore, the faith is the complete New Testament teaching concerning the true Church of Jesus Christ. All believers are evidently in need of exhortations to stand fast in the faith, and to continue therein (I Cor. 16:13; Acts 14:22).

The faith set before us in the Word of God was once for all delivered to the saints. Therefore any claim to further revelation in these last days is in itself an evidence of apostasy. Near the beginning of the Bible, in the heart of the Word of God, and on the last page we find warnings against attempting to add to God's revelation (Deut. 4:2; Prov. 30:6; Rev. 22:18).

The fact that we are living in a time when there are many books which claim to add something to the canon of Scripture is a clear indication that these are indeed the last days. Thank God for the assurance that what was given by the apostles is final: It was once for all delivered to the saints; it is a heritage for which all who love the Lord must contend as long as He gives them breath.

THREE MARKS OF APOSTASY

For there are certain men crept in privily, even they who were of old written of beforehand unto this condemnation, ungodly men, turning the grace of our God into lasciviousness, and denying our only Master and Lord, Jesus Christ (v. 4).

WHY WAS JUDE constrained to write the strange letter which bears his name? Why is it necessary for us to contend earnestly for the faith of our fathers? Here is the answer. Apostates have stealthily crept in among true believers. Satan has sown his tares among the wheat. False brethren have stolen into the Church (Gal. 2:4, 5), imperiling the saints (II Cor. 11:26).

This situation began in Jude's day; it has continued and become worse; it will reach its final consummation when "in the latter times some shall depart from the faith, giving heed to seducing spirits, and doctrines of demons" (I Tim. 4:1). It is written (I Tim. 4:6) that if we put the brethren in remembrance of these things, we shall be good ministers of Jesus Christ. Can a faithful minister of the Lord remain silent in the presence of apostasy, with such verses as these in the Bible?

Jude reminds us that the condemnation of such men was prewritten of old. Enoch prophesied of their doom even before the Flood (vv. 14, 15). There are many other announcements of judgment to come upon all who turn away from what God has said.

The Lord warned of the appearing of these of whom Jude

writes. Satan would come and sow tares while men slept.
He would sow his own men among the people of God,
"children of the wicked one" among the "children of the
kingdom" (Matt. 13:24-30).

Who would have supposed that in pulpits where these
words of Christ were once respected, some would one day
stand and declare that on the contrary, men are really brothers? Christ said there are children of the Devil (John 8:44);
some men say there are none. Who is to be believed? It
is an amazing fact that today the false doctrine of the
universal brotherhood of man is so widely accepted and proclaimed that multitudes think it to be a basic tenet of
Christianity!

Again, who would have imagined that the universal Fatherhood of God would some day be taught where once
men believed the Bible revelation that only those who receive Christ have the right to be called sons of God (John
1:12), that we "are all the children of God by faith in
Christ Jesus" (Gal. 3:26)? Where Christ is denied, or His
teachings thus perverted, there is apostasy. Christ has warned
us; Jude has told us what to do. As we examine ourselves
whether we be in the faith (II Cor. 13:5), we ought to
ask ourselves, Am I contending earnestly for the faith? What
form does my contending take?

There is another parable of Christ which casts brilliant
light upon the difficult doctrine of apostasy. In the parable
of the sower, the seed, and the soils, our Lord revealed
that there is a class of men, likened to seed sown on rocky
ground, who "when they hear, receive the word with joy;
and these have no root, which for a while believe, and in
time of temptation *fall away*" (Luke 8:13). It is significant
that the Holy Spirit led the writer of the third Gospel to
use the verb form of the word *apostasy* to express this idea
of falling away.

An apostate is therefore one who receives the Word, believes it for a time, then falls away. How can this be? One
explanation, apparently overlooked in studies of this subject,
lies in a careful choice of language by the Holy Spirit in

the writing of the three Gospel accounts of the sower. Although stony-ground hearers are said to "receive" the Word (*dekomai,* Luke 8:13), a much stronger term is used of the good-ground hearers (*paradekomai,* Mark 4:20). In contrast with the others, the good-ground group "receives-to-the-side" the Word of the Lord. They welcome it into their hearts.

It should be noted that those who fall away are not said to understand the Word, nor to bring forth fruit (Matt. 13:23). Instead, they do not even have roots. They have no life in Christ. This the Book of Jude confirms by referring to apostates as "without fruit, twice dead, plucked up by the roots" (v. 12).

Apostasy is not to be confused with mere indifference to the Word, nor error or heresy. A born-again person may fall into error, or embrace some heresy; but there seems to be no scriptural warrant for thinking that he may become apostate. An apostate has received light, but not life. He may have received, in some degree, the written Word; but he has not received the living Word, the Son of God.

As Jude makes abundantly clear throughout his epistle, deliberate rejection of the truth after it has first been received is involved in apostasy. "They received not the love of the truth, that they might be saved" (II Thess. 2:10). Judas was an apostate, so were Cain, Balaam, and Korah (v. 11). In Acts 8:13-23, Simon the sorcerer is said to have believed and been baptized, yet he remained in the gall of bitterness and the bond of iniquity.

Our text describes these certain men as having "crept in privily." Literally, the expression may be rendered, "have settled down alongside." They sit with us in our churches, they are alongside of us in our Sunday schools. Peter used a similar word: "There shall be false teachers among you, who *privily shall bring* in damnable heresies, even denying the Lord that bought them" (II Peter 2:1). Jude tells us of men who sneak in among us; Peter speaks of the damnable false doctrine which they stealthily introduce.

Jude 4 gives us an important description of what manner

of men these are. They have three outstanding characteristics. An apostate (1) is ungodly, (2) perverts the grace
of our God into lasciviousness, and (3) denies our only
Master and Lord, Jesus Christ.

The careful student will observe that these three thoughts
reappear elsewhere in Jude. For example, in verse 11, Cain
illustrates the ungodliness of apostasy; Balaam, the perversion of grace into lasciviousness; Korah, the denial of the
divinely ordained pre-eminence of Moses, God's appointed
leader of His people for that time, and a figure of Christ.

An apostate is first of all an *ungodly* man. Thayer's
Lexicon defines the Greek word *asebes* as "destitute of reverential awe toward God." We must not think of open immorality or other wickedness as necessarily a characteristic
of apostasy, but rather a lack of what is called repeatedly
in the Old Testament, "the fear of God," that reverential
awe of Him which leads to implicit obedience to His revealed will. There is a form of godliness which denies the
power thereof (II Tim. 3:5), denies the Gospel of Christ
as the power of God unto salvation (Rom. 1:16), denies
also the transforming power of God which enables a true
believer to live the supernatural life called for by the New
Testament (Phil. 3:10).

An ungodly man, such as Jude describes in this graphic
word-picture, may be a good man in the eyes of other
men. He may not be iniquitous, criminal, or depraved.
Nevertheless, the Bible calls him ungodly, because he lacks
the quality of godliness mentioned some fifteen times in the
Scriptures. Jude is not speaking of outward appearances,
but of the heart (I Sam. 16:7). When the heart does not
accept all of the Word as given by the Lord, the Holy Spirit
labels that heart "ungodly."

It cannot be said of such a man that he "is poor and
of a contrite spirit, and trembleth at my word" (Isa. 66:2).
He may profess belief in God, but he does not believe in
the God of the Bible, the God and Father of our Lord
Jesus Christ. He may speak of God as love, stealing the
phrase from the Bible he despises; but he rejects God's

wrath against sin, God's holiness, God's acceptance of the finished work of Christ on behalf of sinners who otherwise would merit His wrath.

No matter how often the universal Fatherhood of God may be proclaimed as a Christian doctrine, it is not possible to believe God is the Father of all men and at the same time believe also that what Christ said to some men is true, "Ye are of your father the devil." No matter how gifted and persuasive a religious leader may be, we must recognize him as a living example of apostasy, an ungodly man, if he lacks that reverential awe for the God of the Word, and for the Word of God, which has marked the true Church throughout its history.

Second, an apostate changes or perverts the grace of our God into lasciviousness. Perversion of the doctrine of grace is one of the touchstones which indicate a falling away from the truth. Grace is often defined as unmerited favor, or favor granted when judgment has been merited. We are saved by grace, apart from the deeds of the law (Eph. 2:8, 9). When this precious truth of the Bible is perverted into license to sin, apostasy has come in. One of its earmarks is exhibited when a professing Christian thinks he may do as he pleases, go where he pleases, indulge fleshly desires freely, surrender to evil tendencies. Theologians apply the name "antinomianism" to this phenomenon of lawlessness.

It is an interesting fact that the grace of God is said in Titus 2:11-13 to teach us, who possess salvation, to deny ungodliness and worldly lusts, while living soberly, righteously, godly, and in continuous anticipation of the appearing of the Lord Jesus. Thus, it is impossible to pervert the grace of God into lasciviousness without first setting aside a part of what God has revealed about His grace. Apostasy always begins with the rejection of the Word of God. When something is placed above the Word, whether tradition, custom, creed, loyalty to an organization, or anything else, no matter how good in itself, there is at least danger that it may lead to apostasy.

Finally, an apostate denies our only Master and Lord,

Jesus Christ. It is almost startling to read this statement in an epistle written some nineteen hundred years ago, after witnessing the denials which characterize our own generation.

There are four parts to the title of Christ used here. In order, they speak of His universal sovereignty, His position as Lord of the believer's life, His Saviourhood, and His Messiahship. All four are being denied today by "certain men" who have "crept in privily."

Instead of the *Sovereign* of the universe whom angels worship, the Creator and Sustainer of all things, He is represented as a mere man, neither pre-existent nor virgin born. His rightful claim as *Lord* of all true Christians (Acts 10:36) is denied in the rejection of the revealed truth that He rose from the dead "that he might be Lord both of the dead and living" (Rom. 14:9). Although the Scriptures set Him forth as *Jehovah the Saviour,* the very meaning of the name Jesus, it is popular to refer to Him as a human martyr rather than the divine Saviour. As *Christ,* He is the Anointed One of Old Testament prophecy, but modern apostasy sets aside the Old Testament as an untrustworthy patchwork of folklore.

In a peculiar way, the twentieth century in particular seems to be described here, since so many are now characterized by what they deny rather than by what they believe about the Lord Jesus. The apostle's statement in II Peter 2:1, 2 seems already to have had a large measure of fulfillment. False teachers are among us. They have brought in "damnable heresies, even denying the Lord that bought them." Many now follow their pernicious ways. By reason of them the way of truth is evil spoken of.

Little though they heed Him, our Lord said of them: "Whosoever shall deny me before men, him will I also deny before my Father which is in heaven" (Matt. 10:33). To this agree the words of II Timothy 2:12, "If we deny him, he also will deny us." The plain language used by the Holy Spirit ought to rebuke anyone who is timid about unmasking unbelief: "Who is a liar but he that denieth that Jesus is the Christ? He is antichrist, that denieth the

Father and the Son. Whosoever denieth the Son, the same hath not the Father" (I John 2:22, 23).

Denying the Lord that bought them, denying His virgin birth, miracles, substitutionary death, bodily resurrection, promised return; having a form of godliness while denying the power thereof—these are only some of the denials marking men as apostates in our own time.

There seems to be a definite downward progress in verse 4: first, the absence of any real reverence for God and His Word; then a twisting of the blessed doctrine of grace into an excuse for sin; at last an open denial of the Son of God as Saviour and Lord.

Such things begin secretly in an unbelieving, unregenerate heart. They grow on the same stony soil which refuses to allow the Word to take root after it has been sown there. Finally, they break out into the life, and lead to the state described in Titus 1:16: "They profess that they know God; but in works they deny him, being abominable, and disobedient, and unto every good work reprobate." This is a definition of apostasy when it has reached its inevitable final stage. The man who today secretly departs from the truth will ultimately become a living demonstration of the truth of the Word of God.

SAVED AND THEN DESTROYED

Now I desire to put you in remembrance, though ye know all things once for all, that the Lord, having saved a people out of the land of Egypt, afterward destroyed them that believed not (v. 5).

THERE IS NOTHING NEW about departure from the truth of God. It is as old as the history of the human race, for Cain was an apostate (v. 11). The nation Israel, the angels who sinned, and the people of Sodom and Gomorrah are familiar Old Testament examples of a falling away from God. We know these records well enough, but a continuous decay of our knowledge demands that we be reminded of them in view of the coming of apostasy into the professing Church.

Every Bible-believing Christian knows the necessity for daily reading of the Scriptures. God calls upon us to meditate on His Word day and night. If we are to be on guard against spiritual declension, if we are to contend for the faith, we must allow Jude to take us back to the ancient inspired records. They contain lessons we need to learn again and again.

Before we are reminded of individual cases of apostasy (v. 11), we are asked to recall three cases of what might be termed corporate departure from God's revealed will. The first concerns a falling away within the ranks of the people of Israel, who were under the blood of the Passover lamb. The second is taken from the history of sinning angels in the invisible spirit world. The third is found in the story of one of the most wicked groups of beings in all the Bible, the people of Sodom and Gomorrah. Here are representatives of each of the three great classes of God's creatures mentioned in Scripture: saved men, angels, and unsaved men.

What does the Holy Spirit want to teach us by bringing before us the old record of the wilderness experience of the Israelites? Not the fact that God is able and willing to save, important as that is. That He is almighty to deliver is taught again and again from Genesis to Revelation. The Spirit's object here is not to present the blessed truths of the slaying of the Passover lamb and the sprinkling of its blood, or the miracles of the Red Sea and the preservation of a vast host in a howling wilderness; not the typology of the tabernacle, priesthood, and offerings. Whole books are given to these great themes. But Jude writes of Israel's sin and punishment only as it relates to the central subject of his epistle, apostasy.

There is one great lesson for us in verse 5. After God has saved a people for His name, He reserves the right to destroy that people if they become guilty of certain forms of unbelief or other sins to which unbelief leads.

Let us not minimize this plain teaching of the Word of God in our zeal to protect the truth of the grace of God, or the safekeeping of the saints. We would not be put in remembrance of this appalling record if it had no meaning for us. We should be aware of what the Bible teaches about assurance and safekeeping; we may well rejoice in reading our Lord's words, "They shall never perish" (John 10:28); "shall never thirst" (John 4:14). Nevertheless, it is also written "that the Lord, having saved a people out of the land of Egypt, afterward destroyed them that believed not." It behooves us to search the Scriptures as to (1) what this salvation was, (2) what this unbelief was, and (3) what this destruction was.

There can be no doubt that those whom the Lord saved

out of the land of Egypt were truly saved. In announcing
their deliverance, the Lord called Israel "my people" again
and again. He said: "I have surely seen the affliction of my
people that are in Egypt" (Exod. 3:7). He instructed Moses
to say to Pharaoh, "Let my people go" (Exod. 5:1). It is
written: "Happy art thou, O Israel: who is like unto thee,
O people saved by the Lord" (Deut. 33:29). The beautiful
story of the Passover lamb, followed by the manifestation
of God's power as He came down in person to deliver
His people, speak so plainly of Christ, there can be no
doubt but that those who came forth from the land of
Egypt were saved in a deeper sense than mere escape from
the bondage of Egypt.

Without doubt the mixed multitude which came with
them included many unbelievers, but no one would maintain
that all who perished in the wilderness also perished eternally. If this were so then only Caleb and Joshua were true
believers, since they alone of all who crossed the Red Sea,
above twenty years of age, entered the land of promise.

What, then, was the unbelief of which we are reminded
by Jude? It was a falling away from the Shepherd of Israel,
who led Joseph like a flock (Ps. 80:1). The record appears
in Numbers 14. When the report came in from the spies
who searched out the land and found strong enemies en-
trenched therein, "all the congregation lifted up their voice,
and cried; and the people wept that night. And all the
children of Israel murmured against Moses and against
Aaron: and the whole congregation said unto them, Would
God that we had died in the land of Egypt! or would God
we had died in this wilderness!" (Num. 14:1, 2).

By some law of the unseen world (Matt. 12:36), some
unsuspected element in the purpose of God, this cry of unbelief was heard and answered as though it were a prayer.
"As truly as I live, saith the Lord, as ye have spoken in
mine ears, so will I do to you: your carcasses shall fall in
this wilderness; and all that were numbered of you, according to your whole number, from twenty years old and up-

ward, which have murmured against me" (Num. 14:28, 29).

By solemn covenant, Israel had been given the land (Gen. 15:18-21; Num. 13:2). But the faith which had accepted the promise of salvation through the blood of sprinkling failed when confronted with the promise of a life of victory and fruitfulness in the place of God's choosing.

It is one thing to believe and be saved; it is something else to enter the land of promise afterward through believing what God's Word says to those who are under the blood. Some know Jesus as Saviour who do not know Him as Lord. Continuing in His Word after believing on Him makes us "disciples indeed" (John 8:31). There are blessings in this life awaiting all who delight themselves in Him after they have first trusted in Him (Ps. 37:3, 4).

Unbelief kept Israel from enjoying the life of Canaan. "And to whom sware he that they should not enter into his rest, but to them that believed not? So we see that they could not enter in because of unbelief" (Heb. 3:18, 19). We are exhorted to fear lest we likewise fail to enter into God's rest (4:1). The importance of the warning given to the Church in Jude 5 is emphasized by the fact that this sin of Israel is also dealt with at length elsewhere in the New Testament.

In I Corthinthians 10:1-12, Christians are instructed not to be ignorant of these things. They "happened unto them by way of example; and they were written for our admonition, upon whom the ends of the ages are come." Any doubt as to the meaning of Jude 5 is dissolved by this passage.

Five things were true of the Israelites who died in the wilderness. They were all under the cloud; all passed through the sea; all were baptized unto Moses; all ate the same spiritual meat; all drank of the same spiritual drink, "for they drank of that spiritual Rock that followed them: and that Rock was Christ. But with many of them God was not well pleased: for they were overthrown in the wilderness." Five things are then listed against which this great example of unbelief warns us. We should not lust after evil things, be idolaters, commit fornication, tempt Christ, nor murmur.

The conclusion of this account in I Corinthians 10 is given in verse 12: "Wherefore let him that thinketh he standeth take heed lest he fall." It is evidently possible for those whom Paul calls brethren (v. 1) to fall. He does not say they may become apostates; the original word is quite different (being *pipto* rather than *apostasia*). The same Greek root appears also in II Peter 3:17: "Beware lest ye also, being led away with the error of the wicked, fall from your own steadfastness."

Although expositors generally refrain from commenting on the meaning of the warning here given in Jude 5, the fact that I Corinthians 10 and Hebrews 3 and 4 likewise attach great importance to what happened to Israel in the wilderness as an example for Christians, makes certain points unmistakably clear.

According to Jude 5, one may be saved, then become guilty of unbelief, and be judged of God because of it. Paul lists five elements in the common salvation of Israel at the beginning of her wilderness journey, gives five ancient sins born of unbelief which threaten the believer in the present age, and warns of the danger of falling. According to Hebrews 3:12, *the brethren* must beware of "an evil heart of unbelief, in departing from the living God."

What was the destruction visited by the Lord upon the Israelites? There seems to be no basis whatsoever in the context, immediate or remote, for any assumption that it was more than the destruction of the flesh. Israel lost her opportunity for life in the Promised Land, but it is not said that she lost her salvation.

In order to make this clear, let us again recall the references to sin in Jude 5-7, first on the part of God's people Israel, then by angels concerning whom no salvation is mentioned, and finally by unsaved Gentiles.

Of Israel it is simply written that God destroyed them,

but in the other accounts "everlasting chains" and "eternal fire" are mentioned. We have authority to speak of eternal punishment in connection with fallen angels and lost men and women, but we would go beyond what is written if we said the people of Israel who fell in the wilderness were punished with everlasting destruction from the presence of the Lord.

The word *apollumi,* translated "destroyed" in Jude 5, is used elsewhere both of physical death, as in Luke 15:17, and of eternal death, as in John 3:16. In both places it is translated "perish." The context determines the meaning of the word.

Jude is by no means alone in warning of the possibility of the destruction of believers by the Lord if they are guilty of certain sins. In I John 5:16 we find the statement, "There is a sin unto death." This passage may also be rendered, "There is sin unto death." We are not told what the precise nature of such sin is; doubtless it takes many forms. In I Corinthians 11:29, 30 it is revealed that sickness, weakness, and death had come upon those who ate and drank at the Lord's Supper in an unworthy manner. It was sin unto death. It resulted in physical death on the part of some who were called saints (I Cor. 1:2).

Occasionally one hears of cases where believers in our own day apparently sin unto death. Christians in an eastern city thought they had seen an illustration of this when a well-known pastor died after sinning publicly against a church with which he had been connected. We know of a young man who said, not long before his death, that he was convinced he had committed such a sin in giving up the ministry for financial reasons, after having received a definite call to preach the Word.

Whether or not such cases are rightly interpreted as illustrations of I John 5:16, it is a matter of divine revelation that God is now, in the church age, removing some of His people from this scene because of certain sins. This fact is sufficient reason for our taking Jude 5 seriously as a warning against unbelief, lest we be taken away from any further opportunity for serving Christ on earth.

This is not a major doctrine of Scripture, but it is a part of God's revelation for us. Many faithful servants of Christ are called to glory at an early age; we dare not say of any man that he sinned unto death. We must rather see that we ourselves profit by what is written. Jude 5 is given to warn us, not to enable us to judge others.

One individual in Corinth, because of a particular sin, was delivered unto Satan "for the destruction of the flesh, that the spirit may be saved in the day of the Lord Jesus Christ" (I Cor. 5:5). Ananias and Sapphira were struck dead for lying to the Holy Spirit (Acts 5:1-11). Such cases demonstrate the importance of Jude's warning. They show the seriousness of sin on the part of the people of God.

God is faithful. He will not suffer us to be tested beyond our strength. With every testing, a way of escape is provided. We are not left in the dark as to how we are to avoid such a visitation as Jude 5 describes. "If we would judge ourselves, we should not be judged. But when we are judged, we are chastened of the Lord, that we should not be condemned with the world" (I Cor. 11:31, 32).

God has given us His Word. One of its functions is to provide a means of self-judgment. When it reveals that something we contemplate, or something we do, is sin against God, it affords us the opportunity to confess and forsake our sin. We avoid the necessity of judgment from God when we judge ourselves in the light of His Word. Chastening, as divine judgment upon us, may be our portion if we fail to turn aside from that which the Word calls sin.

Ephesians 5:25-27, the best known passage on this subject, speaks of this purifying power of the Bible. Christ loved the Church and gave Himself for it, that He might sanctify and cleanse it with the laver of water in the Word (lit.). In ancient Israel, when there was sin, there was also the laver provided for these who served the tabernacle. Made of brazen mirrors and containing water, it not only revealed the need for cleansing, but also offered the means for that cleansing. In like manner, the Word of God reveals our sin, and provides for our cleansing: "If we confess our sins, he is faithful and just to forgive us our sins, and to cleanse us from all unrighteousness" (I John 1:9).

THE ANGELS WHO SINNED

And angels that kept not their own principality, but left their proper habitation, he hath kept in everlasting bonds under darkness unto the judgment of the great day (v. 6).

WE ARE TAKEN FAR BACK into the ancient past for the second historical example of corporate punishment visited upon those who turned away from revealed truth concerning God's place and purpose for them. The scene changes from the world of men to the angelic realm. There was a time, long ago, when angels kept not their own first estate or principality, but left their proper habitation. These beings are now reserved in everlasting bonds in some dark corner of the universe awaiting the judgment of the terrible day when God will pass final sentence upon them.

When did this angelic apostasy take place? Is anything written about its nature? What important truths does the Holy Spirit mean to convey by bringing such a subject before the saved members of the human race? Such questions are certain to rise in the minds of all who are sincerely desirous of understanding the sacred text.

Three views of the time, place, and nature of the sin in Jude 6 are held by evangelicals. Some maintain that we are not intended to know any more than has been revealed in the brief statement given here. Lenski, for example, assumed that these angels "were dissatisfied, wanted a still higher

domain, not belonging to them, and left their own . . .
habitation—we may say the capital from which they were
designed by God to rule—as not being grand enough for
them. . . . Beyond this we have no light on the sin and
the fall of the angels. We are not to know all about the
devils and their sin, but are to be on our guard against
them" (*Interpretation of Peter, John, and Jude*, p. 630).

Not everyone would agree that Jude actually teaches all
this. Nevertheless, fear of going beyond what is written
causes some to agree that "beyond this [verse] we have no
light," even though such a position almost seems to ignore
a subject introduced into the Bible by the Holy Spirit.

The most serious objection to such an explanation is the
fact that the context does not favor it. Jude 6 stands between
two other illustrations, both of which were taken from the
Old Testament. A knowledge of the Old Testament is required for the proper understanding of verses 5 and 7,
dealing with Israel and Sodom. It does not seem likely that
the second one of three God-given references to historical
examples of apostasy should be entirely without the support
of the sacred writings provided for the other two. Jude is
putting his readers in remembrance of familiar truths. It is
difficult to understand why he should now refer to something they never heard of before, something never mentioned elsewhere in the Bible.

A second explanation is that Jude 6 refers to angels involved in the fall of Lucifer, who became Satan (Isa. 14:12-
17; Ezek. 28:12-19), a sin which swept perhaps one-third
of these beings from their heavenly estate (Rev. 12:4).
Some details of this position, it may be granted, are in
agreement with the Biblical doctrine of Satan, but other
details are not. Therefore the explanation is inacceptable
to most students.

It is certainly true that Satan has his angels, for whom
judgment is reserved. Christ spoke of "fire, prepared for the
devil and his angels" (Matt. 25:41). Satan is called "the

prince of the demons" who make up his kingdom (Matt. 12:24-27, A.S.V.), and some teachers believe the demons are fallen angels, although this is not explicitly taught in the Scriptures.

The great difficulty presented by this second view is the fact that neither Satan's angels nor the demons are now bound (Rev. 12:9; Matt. 10:8). Therefore it is necessary to escape the plain meaning of our text by some such fanciful theory as was first enunciated by Clement of Alexandria: "The chains in which the evil angels are now confined are the air near this earth of ours, and . . . they may well be said to be chained, because they are restrained from recovering the glory and happiness they have lost" (*Lange's Commentary*).

It is not easy to believe that angels said by Jude to be bound in darkness are not really bound at all, but are free in the bright sunlight of our own atmosphere. Therefore a great many expositors today hold the position held by the early church, that Jude 6 refers to Genesis 6:1-4:

> There were giants in the earth in those days; and also after that, when the sons of God came in unto the daughters of men, and they bare children to them, the same became mighty men which were of old, men of renown (Gen. 6:4).

Accepting this view does not mean that we fully understand it, nor that we would be dogmatic about it. Still, an examination of all the evidence in its favor, plus the lack of any other satisfactory explanation of Jude's words, seems to compel a choice between holding the ancient view or none at all.

Several reasons may be cited in favor of our regarding Genesis 6 as the Old Testament record which Jude is bringing to remembrance.

1. At the time this epistle was written, it was commonly believed by the people of Israel that Genesis 6 described a

sin committed by angels who left their own proper habitation to live on earth with the daughters of men. Wrote Josephus, the great Jewish historian and a contemporary of Jude: "Many angels accompanied with women, and begat sons that proved unjust" (*Antiquities 1:3:1*). Whiston comments in a footnote to this passage in his translation of Josephus: "This notion that the fallen angels were, in some sense, the fathers of the old giants was the common opinion of antiquity."

2. The common Bible of the days in which Jude and Josephus wrote was the Septuagint, a Greek translation of the original Hebrew. Where our version reads "sons of God" in Genesis 6:2, 4, the Septuagint reads "angels of God." Just as the readers of this epistle would turn to Genesis 19 for the sin of Sodom, and to Numbers 14 for the sin of Israel, so they would turn to Genesis 6:1-7 for the inspired record of the sin of the angels who departed from their own place.

It cannot be denied that the Hebrew expression rendered "sons of God" in our Bibles is used exclusively of angels elsewhere in the Old Testament. It appears in Job 1:6 and 2:1, where angels are obviously in view. Satan was among them. The Septuagint renders it "angels of God" in these two places also. Even a somewhat similar term found in passages like Psalm 89:6 and Daniel 3:25 does not refer to men. When Israel is spoken of as a son of God in Exodus 4:22 and Isaiah 43:6, a totally different expression is used, and the name for God is changed. Israel is called a son of Jehovah; Genesis 6:2 refers to sons of Elohim.

If we seek to introduce a Greek New Testament phrase referring to men of the new creation (as in John 1:12) into the Hebrew Old Testament in an effort to avoid the early Church's position regarding Genesis 6, we not only violate sound rules of exegesis, we introduce men into Job 38:7, where "all the sons of God shouted for joy" at the primeval creation, when men did not yet exist.

3. The early Church understood that Jude 6 refers to Genesis 6. In fact, it was not until the latter part of the fourth century of the Christian era that any other view was suggested. At that time, Julius Africanus, a contemporary of Origen, enunciated the view which afterward prevailed. He wrote: "What is meant by the Spirit, in my opinion, is that the descendants of Seth are called the sons of God" (*Ante-Nicene Fathers,* vol. 6, p. 131). Eusebius, the great church historian, was one of the men who insisted that the original view of the Church was correct. He compared the narrative of Genesis 6 with stories of Titans and giants in Greek mythology. Celsus, and Julian the apostate, used the older common belief of the Church as a ground for attacking Christianity. Cyril of Alexandria, in his reply felt obliged to repudiate the orthodox position as unworthy, and adopted the new position suggested by Africanus.

Old writers such as Justin, Athenagoras, and Cyprian held the position that angels are referred to in Genesis 6, while the Sethite interpretation prevailed in the Middle Ages. Yet, as Alford has pointed out, "there is nothing in the context to suggest this, no sign that the Sethites were distinguished for piety; they are not even exempted from the charge of general wickedness which brought on the flood."

4. The context of Genesis 6:2, 4 favors the interpretation held by the early Church and the Jews. There was something strange and terrible in those ancient unions, because their progeny were monstrous. This is a fact difficult to explain if the text refers merely to godly men taking ungodly wives. (The text does not say, nor imply, that these "daughters of men" were ungodly.)

"There were giants in the earth in those days; and also after that, when the sons of God came in unto the daughters of men, and they bare children to them." These giants are said to have appeared on two different occasions, before the Flood and "also after that." The word rendered "giants" does, in point of fact, occur only once after the record of the Flood, and that is in Numbers 13:33. It is *Nephilim* in the Hebrew, meaning literally "the fallen ones." It was translated "giants" in the Septuagint and the English Bible for the reason, undoubtedly, that these beings were gigantic in stature. The bedstead of one of them (at their second appearance in history) was more than thirteen feet long (Deut. 3:11). The men of Israel were as grasshoppers before them (Num. 13:33; cf., Amos 2:9).

On the first appearance of these monstrous beings upon the earth, God destroyed them in the Flood. When a second group of them appeared, He ordered His people to destroy them. Why does the text call them "the fallen ones"? Jude would seem to have the answer. He is writing of apostasy, which means a falling away. He is also writing of fallen angels, and here in the Old Testament is a record believed for many centuries to speak of fallen angels, and of other strange beings in the earth linked to them, and given the name of *fallen ones*, whom God ordered destroyed. This must be more than coincidence, and it is significant that immediately after Jude referred his readers to the apostasy of Numbers 14, he spoke of the other apostasy mentioned in Numbers 13, the only other passage in the Hebrew Scriptures which mentions by name the *Nephilim* of Genesis 6:4.

Higher critics, no friends to evangelical teaching, acknowledge the ancient view of Genesis 6. Wrote Driver: "We must see in it an ancient Hebrew legend . . . the intention of which was to account for the origin of a supposed race of prehistoric giants." Joseph B. Mayor, who held higher critical opinions, made a similar admission, calling them "children of heaven and earth, who rose up in insurrection against the gods and were hurled down to Tartarus" (*Jude and II Peter*).

Although space does not permit further discussion of this interesting and terrifying subject, attention is directed to the parallel verse in II Peter 2:4. The original language states that God hurled these sinning angels down into pits of darkness called Tartarus, a region in the unseen world. The language used by Peter depicts dark underground caverns, where the fallen angels now await their final judgment. Somewhere beneath our feet lies a subterranean region where God is keeping these creatures who apostatized from Him, until the great day when they will render an accounting for their sin, whatever it was.

5. The language of Jude 7 seems to require the ancient view of verse 6. The people of Sodom and Gomorrah are said to have gone after strange flesh in like manner as these angels. Alford's comment is typical of the conclusions of many Greek scholars: "In like manner to these . . . the angels above mentioned. The manner was similar, because the angels committed fornication with another race than themselves" (*Greek New Testament*).

It is useless to speculate on the nature of this union. Whether it was brought about by something akin to demon possession, or whether angels have power permanently to assume the form of men is not revealed. We actually know very little about the nature of angels. They have walked the earth in what appeared to be human form, so that believers and unbelievers both referred to them as men (Gen. 19:5, 10, 16). They spoke as men, took men by the hand, and even ate men's food (Gen. 18:8; 19:3, 16). Who then can assert that angels could not leave their proper habitation and dwell on the earth?

The only verse cited to support the position that Genesis 6:1-4 cannot refer to angels is Matthew 22:30: "For in the resurrection they neither marry, nor are given in marriage, but are as the angels of God in heaven." But Genesis 6 does not speak of the angels of God in Heaven. What may now be true of them was not necessarily true of fallen angels on earth in the days of Noah. We do not know enough about the nature of angels to be dogmatic about what they can or cannot do. If we reject the interpretation of the early

Church, we should recognize that it is not because we have come into possession of facts unknown to the early Church. If anything, believers in apostolic days knew more than we do. Not one new fact concerning Jude 6 has been turned up since then.

In addition to these five compelling reasons for holding this third view of the passage before us may be mentioned the utter absence of any other Old Testament record of an angelic sin such as Jude describes, and the strong confirmatory value of heathen writings which undoubtedly owe their origin to the Bible record. Mythology contains accounts of "gods" who came down to earth from Heaven and produced a race of heroes or men of renown. The subject is developed in *The Fallen Angels and the Heroes of Mythology*, by John Fleming.

What are the lessons this record is intended to convey? Doubtless we would be warranted in drawing many conclusions not directly related to the central theme of Jude. Some of these, found in James M. Gray's *Spiritism and the Fallen Angels*, and in Pember's *Earth's Earliest Ages*, deals with the dangers attending traffic with the unseen world. A large body of Scripture warns men against meddling with the world of spirits, but this is not the subject of our epistle.

One purpose of this revelation of the punishment overtaking the angels who sinned is certainly to emphasize the serious nature of apostasy. Beings of a higher order than ours were hurled down to a dark place of confinement, where they have remained for thousands of years. God has not changed His attitude toward them; time has not mitigated the seriousness of their sin. They are bound with "everlasting bonds." Their future is one of judgment, not mercy.

Remembering this, we cannot think lightly of apostasy in any form. The evil men of whom Jude writes, who have crept into the church by stealth, are prewritten unto condemnation. Like the angels, they knew and turned away from the truth of God and the place God had purposed they should occupy. If we who know and obey the truth are warned, how much more should men and women who have apostatized from the truth take heed before they are overtaken by the announced condemnation!

Another practical lesson to be found in this record, as we place it alongside the story of Israel's destruction, is that judgment may be executed speedily when apostasy has come in. There is a sin unto death. It has happened to God's ancient people; it has happened to angels. God has suddenly brought to an end further opportunity to enjoy the blessings of life in the time He has given before eternity dawns. God declares that He will do this again.

The angels' doom is sealed. They cut themselves off from everything that might have been theirs had they continued subject to their Creator. Likewise, the Israelites had the Promised Land before them, with eternal riches doubtless to be won for faithful service therein. They lost it all through unbelief.

It is possible for Christians to suffer loss both in this life and in the life to come, if they fall away into sin which God cannot tolerate. Only eternity can reveal the incalculable difference between the eternal state of those who have been faithful unto death, and those who have acted so as to deprive themselves of rewards they might otherwise have earned.

We realize further, as we meditate upon what is before us in Jude 6, that a great day of judgment is coming. Christians must all appear before the judgment seat of Christ. Unsaved men and women also face an inevitable hour of accounting. Just as the fallen angels are helpless to change one iota of what they did before the unannounced moment when God took them away, so it will be too late for men to repent of apostasy or other sin, when God's time has come for the end of their lives on earth.

Darkness is ahead for some; light is ahead for others. Everlasting bonds and everlasting fire are set over against everlasting liberty and everlasting glory. Trembling and fear is the portion of the ungodly who await judgment; joy unspeakable and full of glory is even now the experience of all who love and obey the Word of God. God is no respecter of persons. He did not respect the persons of angels who once sang His praises. He will not respect men who heed not the message He has given through His servant Jude.

THE DESTRUCTION OF SODOM

*Even as Sodom and Gomorrah, and the cities about them,
having in like manner with these given themselves over to
fornication and gone after strange flesh, are set forth as an
example, suffering the punishment of eternal fire* (v. 7).

I T IS A VERY SOLEMN THING that Sodom and Gomorrah
should be set forth in the Bible as examples for the instruction of the Church. What can believers learn from the
record of the old cities of the plain which God destroyed
because of their terrible wickedness?

One of the most obvious reasons we are put in remembrance of this Bible account of sin and judgment is that it is
prophetic of the apostasy within Christendom in the last days.
Apostates are said by Jude to "turn the grace of our God
into lasciviousness" (v. 4), to "defile the flesh" (v. 8), to
corrupt themselves as beasts (v. 10), and to "walk after their
their own lusts" (v. 16).

We would hardly use such strong language in connection
with the falling away which has progressed so rapidly in our
generation toward its announced climax, but this is the terminology of the Holy Spirit. Christ foretold that the last days
would be as the days of Lot (Luke 17:28-30). Conditions
such as obtained in ancient Sodom will have their counterpart in Christendom just before the Lord returns, as pro-
fessed believers fall into sins which should not even be
named among true followers of Christ (Eph. 5:3).

The twentieth century has witnessed such a renewed outbreak of ancient sins and perversions that even worldly-wise

leaders stand aghast. Headlines concerning crime and immorality in every city of America warn us that we must take a far more literal view of the Book of Jude than has been common in the past. Apostasy may begin with intellectual doubts, but it is certain to end in physical degradation.

In addition to the prophetic character of these passages, other striking spiritual truths of importance to the believer are to be found in Jude 7 and 8. Since Sodom and Gomorrah are mentioned in connection with apostasy, the inference is that the people of these cities were guilty of this great sin. Such, indeed, was the case. Wicked as they were at the time they were destroyed, they once had a knowledge of the truth.

God's original revelation of His holy character was still preserved in Lot's day and was known in the wicked cities of the plain. Only 450 years had passed, according to Ussher's chronology, between the Flood and the overthrow of Sodom. Shem, Noah's son, still walked the earth, having fifty years of life yet before him.

As clearly stated in Romans 1:18-32, when men who once knew God fail to glorify Him, they become vain in their reasoning, and their foolish hearts are darkened. Then God gives them up to uncleanness, vile affections, and a reprobate mind. This was true in Sodom. It will be true within Christendom, as Jude is increasingly illustrated in the days immediately preceding the coming of our Lord.

"Remember Sodom!" writes Jude. As we turn to the record God has given, we remember that Christ was referring to the destruction of Sodom when He said, "Remember Lot's wife" (Luke 17:32). Just before this He had declared: "He that is in the field, let him likewise not return back" (v. 31). Lot's wife is an example of turning back, and turning back is apostasy.

The escaping woman had tasted of deliverance from a place under doom from God. She had followed the word of the Lord, given through angels, almost to the heights where perfect safety lay, when she turned back. Like Israel in the wilderness, and the angels who sinned, she did not have an-

other opportunity to sin against the light which had been
given her. "If any man draw back, my soul shall have no
pleasure in him," declare the Scriptures. "But we are not of
them who draw back . . . but of them that believe to the
saving of the soul" (Heb. 10:38, 39).

The very longsuffering of God, who is not willing that any
should perish, leads some men to harden their hearts and
miss altogether the lesson of these examples cited by Jude.
"Because sentence against an evil work is not executed
speedily, therefore the heart of the sons of men is fully set
in them to do evil" (Eccles. 8:11).

Thank God, He does not deal with everyone as He has
dealt with Israel, the angels, and Sodom. People who turn
back from sure deliverance are not often struck down by
divine judgment as was Lot's wife. Again and again the
grace of God woos us to Himself, though we often turn
away. But it will not always be so. The day of the Lord will
come, as a thief in the night. Let all beware of presuming
too long. The fate of Lot's wife is a lesson for us.

Sodom itself also illustrates an important truth. When
God's Word is too long neglected or resisted, He sends judi-
cial blindness. Sins once abhorred come in where the grace
of God is cast out. There is a state of mind where belief in
the truth is no longer possible. "They could not believe,
because that Isaiah said again, He hath blinded their eyes,
and hardened their heart" (John 12:39, 40).

"Remember Sodom!" says Jude, and we think of Lot,
whose days were so much like the days when the Son of God
is to come again. His entire history is a somber story given
for our admonition.

In the first Bible reference to Sodom and Gomorrah they
are said to have been "in the border of the Canaanites"
(Gen. 10:19). The next mention of these cities reveals that
Lot chose the locality as his dwelling place. He elected to live
a borderline life, as close as possible to the wicked Canaanites, from whom he should have kept himself separate.

Quickly Lot's sorrowful history is told. First he "lifted up his eyes and beheld" the region, which definitely had attractions appealing to the flesh (Gen. 13:10). Then he "chose him all the plain of Jordan" (13:11), although this meant separation from Abraham, the man of God. Next we read that Lot "pitched his tent toward Sodom" (v. 12). Evidently he became a well-known man in that city, because he "sat in the gate" (19:1).

His effort to lead a righteous life there was a matter of contempt to his companions (19:9), and he lost his testimony completely (19:14). His wife perished when she turned back to the doomed place to which he had introduced her; his daughters adopted the morals of the city in which they grew up. Lot himself was saved, yet so as by fire. The last mention of him in the Genesis account shows him dwelling in a dark cave in misery and sin (Gen. 19:30, ff.).

In bright contrast is the story of Abraham, who chose to abide in the heights of Hebron, which means "communion." Long after Lot has passed from view in the sacred record, Abraham is seen communing with the Lord, an example of the life of faith and trust which has strengthened the hearts of believers for four thousand years since then.

We cannot think of Sodom without remembering that the first intercessory prayer of the Bible preceded its destruction (Gen. 18). God revealed to Abraham His purpose to destroy the wicked cities of the plain. The announcement of coming judgment upon the ungodly made Abraham an intercessor at once. He drew near to God and asked for mercy on Sodom, which was going on about its daily business, heedless of its fate.

Destruction was certain, but when judgment was about to descend, "God remembered Abraham, and sent Lot out of the midst of the overthrow" (Gen. 19:29). There was deliverance in answer to the prayer of one righteous man. It was Abraham in the place of communion whom God remembered, not Lot in the place of compromise.

Where God is withholding judgment from any city or nation today, there are righteous men and women praying

for the ungodly. Effectual, fervent prayer ever avails to bring
salvation to individuals living in a world facing inevitable
judgment. God is seeking intercessors like Abraham. "I
sought for a man among them, that should make up the
hedge, and stand in the gap before me for the land, that I
should not destroy it: but I found none" (Ezek. 22:30).
Jeremiah was told: "Run ye to and fro through the streets
of Jerusalem, and see now, and know, and seek in the broad
places thereof, if ye can find a man, if there be any that
executeth judgment, that seeketh the truth; and I will pardon
it" (Jer. 5:1).

This great truth must not be overlooked as we heed the
admonition to remember Sodom. Intercessory prayer is still
necessary if God is to save some out of the fiery judgment
which must eventually fall upon all the ungodly.

Nor dare we neglect the other truth which Lot illustrates,
of salvation "so as by fire," wherein there is the loss of all
else. When our foundation is properly laid, "which is Jesus
Christ," we must be careful how we build upon it. Some
work in gold, silver, precious stones; others in wood, hay,
stubble. Every man's work shall be made manifest. If it has
been like Lot's work, it "shall be burned, he shall suffer loss:
but he himself shall be saved; yet so as by fire" (I Cor.
3:11-15).

"Remember Sodom!" writes Jude, and we ponder the
revelation that these cities, so long ago destroyed, "are set
forth for an example, suffering the punishment of eternal
fire." The literal fire which fell from Heaven bears some
relation to everlasting fire prepared for the Devil and his
angels.

Geologists tell us much about what may have happened
during those terrible hours before Abraham "looked toward
Sodom and Gomorrah . . . and beheld and, lo, the smoke
of the country went up as the smoke of a furnace" (Gen.
19:28).

Dr. Melvin Grove Kyle, famous archaeologist and an
evangelical believer, led an expedition to a site at the south-

ern end of the Dead Sea where the ancient name *Sodom* is preserved in a place called *Jebel Usdum,* or Mount Sodom. He tells us in *Explorations in Sodom* how he found ruins of an old city of Canaan definitely identified as Zoar, on an elevation toward the east (Gen. 19:20-22, 30). As he studied the area, Dr. Kyle concluded that the ruins of Sodom now lie beneath the waters near the shore of the Dead Sea. As silt has been deposited in the north by the Jordan River, the water has gradually encroached upon the southern bank, covering the site where stood the ancient cities of Sodom, Gomorrah, Admah, and Zeboim.

This entire area is a burned-out region of oil and bitumen. Genesis 11:3 and 14:10 are said to have supplied the clue to the presence of oil which led to the discovery of the great Near Eastern oil fields, for the Hebrew word rendered "slime" in those passages is really "bitumen." Old descriptions of the Dead Sea refer to the presence of floating masses of bitumen on its surface.

A great rupture in the earth's strata, dating from Zoar's day, and the presence of vast quantities of sulphur and salt scattered over the region as though by a tremendous cataclysm have led geologists to conclude that there was once a terrific explosion in a subterranean pool of oil near the southern shore of the Dead Sea. As the gas somehow became ignited, the resulting blast lifted a whole section of the floor of the valley into the air. Large quantities of burning oil and sulphur (brimstone), together with salt and bitumen, were showered over the area, destroying whatever they fell upon. In one brief hour, four cities were overwhelmed. They perished as "the Lord rained upon Sodom and upon Gomorrah brimstone and fire from the Lord out of heaven" (Gen. 19:24). According to this explanation, Lot's wife may have been caught in a torrential downpour of salt as she lingered behind her husband, forming a nucleus around which drifts formed a "pillar" of salt.

Whether or not we accept these remarkable conclusions of geology as an explanation of the means God may have em-

ployed in destroying Sodom, it is certain that literal fire did
fall upon that city some four thousand years ago. Why, then,
does Jude 7 speak of Sodom and Gomorrah and the cities
about them as even now "suffering the punishment of eternal
fire"?

The answer is that the ungodly enter fiery torment immediately after death. Christ taught this in Luke 16:19-31,
where a man is described as "tormented in this flame" after
he died. His body is said to have been buried, but he continued in a state of conscious misery. Jude declares that the
inhabitants of Sodom are another example for the instruction of God's people. Being dead for four thousand years,
they have known the punishment of eternal fire all that time.
The lake of fire is the final destiny of all such despisers of
the goodness of God, but there is also an intermediate state,
place, and time of woe.

Nearly two thousand years have passed since Jude by
inspiration wrote of Sodom's punishment. The Spirit-given
words still stand; they are the truth of God. Unbelievers give
them no heed. But they are not given to unbelievers; they are
addressed to us who are beloved, kept, and called.

Unless we remember these words, we shall lack the incentive they should give us to become earnest soul-winners.
We may be living close to the time when the present day of
grace will close. Then it will be too late for all who "received
not the love of the truth, that they might be saved" (II Thess.
2:10). All will be condemned who "believed not the truth,
but had pleasure in unrighteousness" (v. 12). We are their
only hope. Let us, like Abraham, intercede for them and
seek their salvation by every means at our disposal. Otherwise, the smoke of their torment will rise up forever and
ever (Rev. 19:3).

We think of Sodom as guilty of terrible wickedness, but
there is something far worse. It is rejecting the Son of God,
despising the blood which He shed for our salvation.

Sodom and Gomorrah and the cities about them which
followed their evil example still face the day of judgment.

The eternal fire in which they now are being punished will then be exchanged for the lake of fire. But their judgment will be more tolerable than the judgment of your city and mine, if they do not hear the message which we have from God (Luke 10:12). To hear and then to turn away is apostasy from the truth, more awful in the sight of God, than to live as did those cities which had to be destroyed by fire from Heaven as an example for all who should afterward live upon the earth.

ANCIENT SINS REAPPEAR

Yet in like manner these also in their dreamings defile the flesh, and set at nought dominion, and rail at dignities (v. 8).

THREE TIMES Jude has taken us back into the Old Testament to remind us of familiar examples of apostasy upon which God has visited judgment in ancient times. Three case histories have been placed before us, three cameos of wrath against this particular kind of sin, where there has been a falling away from the truth of God. Each of them illustrates, as no other record could, certain aspects of the theme which the Holy Spirit is unfolding.

When the three are taken together, as they are in verse 8, they set forth three characteristics of apostasy as Jude knew it in his day, and as the Church will know it in the last days before the Lord comes "to execute judgment upon all."

An apostate, when he has reached the inevitable end of the path upon which he has embarked, defiles the flesh "in like manner" with the people of Sodom. He sets at nought dominion, as did the angels who despised God's regulations which had placed them in their own principality. He rails at dignities, like the people of Israel who murmured against Moses and Aaron.

Let us recognize at once that all of these marks of full-blown apostasy are not necessarily apparent in every man who has fallen away from the truths he once knew. However, we shall certainly err if we depend upon appearances rather than upon what the Word of God says about the desperately wicked human heart (Jer. 17:9). When an apostate religious

leader stands forth to preach a message of goodness and
social uplift, the world may look upon him as a man of upright character who abhors fleshly lusts. This may actually
be true in fact as well as in appearance.

But when such a man has publicly denied our only Master
and Lord, Jesus Christ, has set at nought His authority, has
"railed at dignities," he has divorced himself from the only
power which can effectually control his lower nature. It is
written that a defiling of the flesh is one of the things which
accompanies the rejection of the truth. Those who study
God's Word know that apostates will ultimately come to
fleshly sin if they have not already. Those who scoff at the
truth of the Bible in the last days are to be, according to
Peter, men "walking after their own lusts" (II Peter 3:3).

True faith in Christ is manifested in a walk which is not
after the flesh, but after the Spirit (Rom. 8:4). Faith leads
to good works. The fruit produced by the Holy Spirit includes godly self-control (Gal. 5:22, 23).

On the other hand, as we see in such passages as Jude 8,
a turning away from the truth of God's Word produces evil
results, not only in the spirit and the soul, but in the body
as well. "Now the works of the flesh are manifest, which are
these; Adultery, fornication, uncleanness, lasciviousness,
idolatry, witchcraft, hatred, variance, emulations, wrath,
strife, seditions, heresies, envyings, murders, drunkenness,
revelings, and such like" (Gal. 5:19-21). Our Saviour
taught that these things proceed out of the heart and defile
a man (Matt. 15:19, 20).

There is nothing pleasant about this terrible description of
all that is actually involved in apostasy, but it is a part of the
eternal Word of God and therefore must be believed. Men
who deny the Lord that bought them may be able to hide
the awful works of the flesh from the public, but they cannot
hide them from God, who has been pleased to reveal them
to His people.

Such persons, we are told, also "set at nought dominion."
The words of verse 4, "denying our only Master and Lord,"

show that verse 8 has primary reference to the setting aside
of Christ as Lord and Master. It is not to be expected that
men who have denied the eternal pre-existence, the virgin
birth, the miracles, the substitutionary death, the resurrection and the return of the Lord Jesus Christ should be willing
to own Him as Lord. "No man can say that Jesus is the Lord,
but by the Holy Ghost" (I Cor. 12:3). These men of whom
Jude writes cannot own Jesus as Lord because they have
not the Spirit (v. 19).

Even though our Lord now permits this denial of His
authority, it is God's ultimate purpose "that at the name of
Jesus every knee should bow . . . and that every tongue
should confess that Jesus Christ is Lord, to the glory of God
the Father" (Phil. 2:10, 11). It is indeed a privilege volun-
tarily to accord Him pre-eminence in everything today when
He is so widely rejected, and before Isaiah 45:23 is fulfilled
in judgment on His enemies.

Without doubt, the setting aside of the authority of the
Word of God is likewise embraced in this comprehensive
revelation given through Jude. The world has indeed seen
the Bible cast aside by apostates and displaced as the one
authoritative rule of faith and life. Once respected creeds
and confessions based upon the authority of God's Word
have likewise been set at nought.

Hand in hand with this rejection of the authority of the
Scripture has gone the demand for a new social order. Thus
the phrase, "set at nought dominion," in Jude 8 supplies a
key to the otherwise inexplicable fact that apostate religious
leaders are often found associated with subversive organizations which seek to overthrow the authority of the United
States. Not until the tide of apostasy began to rise during the
twentieth century was there any serious effort to set aside the
dominion of the government which our fathers established.
Yet it was written nineteen hundred years ago that apostates
would follow such a course.

It is the nature of apostasy to despise dominion. Is this not
one of the "doctrines of demons" to which men will give

heed in the last days? "Now the Spirit speaketh expressly, that in the latter times some shall depart from the faith, giving heed to seducing spirits, and doctrines of demons" (I Tim. 4:1). The danger to our nation in the present century does not spring from those who are faithful to the Word of God. It does come from those who deny our most holy faith.

As we meditate upon the three notable phrases of Jude 8, it is necessary to remind ourselves that we are reading, not of what might be called the people of the world, but rather of those who have crept into the Church. There is much revealed about conditions among men in general in the last days of which Jude writes. There is a "mystery of lawlessness" always present in the world (II Thess. 2:7), destined to break forth into great wickedness when God has withdrawn the restraint He has imposed for the present age. Such lawlessness has its counterpart within the professing Church, when men set at nought Christ's dominion, which has been respected throughout the centuries. The present denial of His Lordship is another indication that His coming draweth nigh.

Finally, apostates are said to "rail at dignities." There might be some difficulty in understanding what is the mind of the Spirit in this phrase were it not for the fact that the same word appears also in verse 9, and again in verse 10. It is translated "speak evil" in the Authorized Version; it might also be rendered "revile."

The illustration given in verse 9 teaches us that one meaning of the phrase "rail at dignities" is the practice of speaking in judgment of someone in a place of authority. This is sin, even though that someone is clearly in the wrong; even though that someone is the Devil himself. Michael, the archangel, would not be guilty of it, but those who apostatize from the truth are characterized by it.

Just as other marks of apostasy are found in lesser degree among true believers as the days darken and the coming of Christ draws on apace, so we find widespread criticism today of men whom God has put in places of authority and leadership. Although the Word says, "Speak evil of no man" (Titus 3:2), the work of God continues to suffer from evil speaking, false accusations, unverified rumors, whisperings, by those who profess to obey the Word. Satan is called the accuser of the brethren (Rev. 12:10). Christians are doing the Devil's work every time they open their mouths against the Lord's chosen vessels.

The language of Jude 8 is here again purposely framed in such general terms as to have wide meaning. Who are the "dignities" against whom apostasy lifts its voice in railing judgment? The supreme dignity being made the target of the fiery darts of unbelief is, of course, the Lord Jesus Christ.

Never before has there been such a concentrated assault upon the Person of Christ, as has been unleashed within the present century in the religious press and in the spoken utterances of many religious leaders. Men rail not only against the deity of the Prince of glory; they speak out against what is written about His holy birth, openly scoff at what He said about the purpose of His death, oppose the truth of nearly every other historic basis of Christianity.

If we were to look for further illustrations of the truth of this third characteristic of apostasy, we would find widespread ridiculing even of the existence of the personal Devil, who is revealed in the Bible as the god of this world. We would find Moses called a man who could not even write; Isaiah scoffingly given the name "Deutero-Isaiah"; Daniel described as a man who never even existed; the writers of the Gospels accused of falsehood; the apostle Paul referred to as a false teacher. Men and institutions truly honoring and obeying God in this generation are attacked and accused of all manner of evil. Surely this third phrase of Jude 8 has been sufficiently vindicated in recent years to suggest that the complete fulfillment of all Jude wrote may be near.

Noteworthy is the truth that it is "in their dreamings" that apostates commit these three sins. It is written in verse 10 that they know not the things they speak against. They are asleep to a whole world of truth. "They that sleep, sleep in the night" (I Thess. 5:7).

We are reminded of one outstanding ecclesiastical leader who decided to devote his life to helping bring about the end of "a divided Protestantism." He gave no heed to those who called his attention to the fact that the Bible does speak about a future world religion, but describes it as an apostate organization.

This man turned away from his primary responsibility to the Lord, and gave himself to his dream of a world church. He even called it a dream, but gave to it his best energies. Ultimately he stood openly with known apostates against the authority of the Scriptures.

Jude seems to share the amazement we all feel as we behold the blindness of unbelief, the folly of apostasy. Others have been punished by the Lord, we are reminded in verses 5-7, *yet* these in their dreamings follow the same evil course. Israel turned away from truths they once believed, to revile Moses and Aaron, and perished in the wilderness, *yet* these men revile dignities. The angels despised the Lord's authority, and were cast down to Tartarus, *yet* these men are following their example by despising dominion. The people of Sodom defiled the flesh, suffering the judgment of eternal fire, *yet* these men have entered upon the same pathway.

It is astonishing, incredible, yet it is true. Let all who are still faithful to the Word of God in these days read and meditate upon the record. Let him who thinketh he standeth take heed lest he also fall.

MICHAEL AND THE DEVIL

But Michael the archangel, when contending with the devil he disputed about the body of Moses, durst not bring against him a railing judgment, but said, The Lord rebuke thee (v. 9).

IT IS A CURIOUS FACT that it is almost impossible to find a sermon or a published article on this strange dispute which once took place between the chief of the holy angels and the chief of wicked spirits. Without doubt, this is because the verse presents a number of difficulties. Nevertheless it is one of the great texts of Scripture condemning those railing judgments by which some, supposing they are manifesting a high degree of spirituality or discernment, speak out against Christian leaders or Christian organizations to call attention to their failings and offer criticism. One of the most disliked commands of the Word of God, and therefore one of the most disobeyed, is this: "Speak evil of no man" (Titus 3:2).

The Holy Spirit has just mentioned (v. 8) three outstanding marks of apostasy: defiling the flesh, despising dominion, and railing at dignities. Although each of the three is illustrated by an example of corporate apostasy from the Old Testament in Jude 5, 6, and 7, and by an example of individual apostasy in verse 11, the subject of railing judgment is considered important enough to merit further illustration, even though this means the introduction of a revelation given nowhere else in the Bible. Undoubtedly, Christendom would witness far less of what may be called "the accusing of the brethren" if Jude 9 were more widely known and honored.

Two mighty angels once disputed over the body of a creature of a lower order than they. The angel who was faithful to his Creator said nothing against his evil opponent, even though he himself was doing the work of God in obedience to a divine command, and even though the Devil who opposed him was seeking to thwart God's purposes! What a rebuke this is for those who boldly and in the name of the Lord speak out in judgment against others!

The apparent problems of Jude 9 ought not to make us turn away from it as something about which it is useless or presumptuous to have an opinion. We are not required to know more than has been revealed about Michael and Satan, but we are expected to know what has been disclosed, and to learn such lessons as are contained therein.

This verse is not said to call to remembrance well-known truths, as are the illustrations cited earlier. It is a new revelation, not previously written with the pen of inspiration, like the prophecy of Enoch recorded in Jude 14, 15. This should not surprise us. Paul quotes words of Christ not found in the Gospels (Acts 20:35). He also mentions the names of two of the magicians in Egypt, although the recorded history of Moses is silent on the subject (II Tim. 3:8). James 5:17 informs us that Elijah prayed that it might not rain for three and one-half years, and faith accepts the fact without question, even though I Kings 17:1 and 18:1 do not reveal that the prayers of the prophet had anything to do with the long drought in Ahab's reign.

There is no record in the Bible to tell us when the incident of Jude 9 took place, where it happened or why. However, there are Scriptures dealing with Michael the archangel and his ministry, the Devil and his objectives, and the disposition of Moses' body when he died. Without presuming to go beyond what is written, we may at least come to an intelligent understanding of some of the principles involved in the struggle to which Jude introduces us.

Michael is the archangel, a term meaning "chief angel," and never used except in the singular, implying that there is only one such being. The name Michael means "who is like unto God?" It speaks of the reverential awe with which he has always served his Creator. This is in striking contrast with the name Satan, which means "adversary," a term descriptive of his antagonism to God.

The first reference in the Bible to Michael by name is in Daniel 10:13. The prophet had been praying for three weeks, when an angel came and told him that the answer to his prayer had been delayed by "the prince of the kingdom of Persia," one of the evil angelic principalities and powers which rule the darkness of this world (Eph. 6:12). The holy angel's message for Daniel was held up until "lo, Michael, one of the chief princes, came to help me." The marginal reading here is, "The first of the chief princes."

A significant fact in this record is that Michael was God's agent for the defeating of Satan's purpose against God's earthly people Israel. This same truth appears in Daniel 10:21, where the archangel is called "Michael your prince" in a message addressed to Daniel. Likewise in Daniel 12:1 we read: "And at that time shall Michael stand up, the great prince which standeth for the children of thy people."

There is another important reference in Scripture to this being. In connection with the same period of tribulation described in Daniel 12:1, and in a context dealing with Israel in the days of her future persecution, it is written: "And there was war in heaven: Michael and his angels fought against the dragon; and the dragon fought and his angels, and prevailed not; neither was their place found any more in heaven. And the great dragon was cast out, that old serpent, called the Devil, and Satan, which deceiveth the whole world: he was cast out into the earth, and his angels were cast out with him" (Rev. 12:7-9).

These several verses reveal two facts which ought to be in our thinking as we meditate on Jude 9. First, Satan seeks to defeat God's program by deception. Second, Michael is

God's chosen instrument for overcoming Satan's purpose regarding Israel. Do these revealed truths cast any light upon this angelic contest about which God has been pleased to speak?

There is a very ancient suggestion as to why the Devil would be interested in the body of Moses. Josephus wrote that Moses "exceeded all men that ever were in understanding . . . he was also such a general of an army as is seldom seen, as well as such a prophet as was never known, and this to such a degree, that whatsoever he pronounced, you would think you heard the voice of God Himself." Even those who did not know Moses "had a strong desire after him" as they perused his laws following his death (*Antiquities of the Jews*, IV:8:49).

Satan has always tried to defeat the worship of the true God. He has filled the world with counterfeits. He has deceived multitudes into venerating relics of saints, so that men prostrate themselves before such things as human hair, bones, and rotten bits of clothing. He has deceived Russia into giving superstitious reverence to the body of Lenin. He will some day bring about the worldwide worship of the beast "wounded to death" (Rev. 13:3, 4). It would be in keeping with his purpose and strategy if he sought to deceive Israel by causing the veneration of the body of Moses, in an effort to destroy obedience to the prophet like unto Moses foretold in Deuteronomy 18:15, 19.

Whether or not we find value in this view, it does have the advantage of suggesting why God buried Moses' body and kept the place of his sepulcher secret, why Satan should have been interested in the body of a man, and why Michael should have opposed the Devil's purpose.

It is a notable fact that of more than five hundred Old Testament references to Moses, only one can be said to refer primarily to *the body* of Moses. It is found in Deuteronomy 34:5, 6: "So Moses the servant of the Lord died there in the land of Moab, according to the word of the Lord. And he buried him in a valley in the land of Moab,

over against Beth-peor: but no man knoweth of his sepulcher unto this day." A dispute over his body would presum-
ably have to take place soon after its burial by the Lord,
before its dissolution.

In the *Targum of Jonathan*, on Deuteronomy 34:6, it is
stated that the grave of Moses was given into the special
custody of Michael. Ancient Jewish traditions speak of a
contest about Moses' soul at the time of his burial.

"According to Oecumenius, the tradition ran that God
had charged Michael the archangel with the burial of Moses;
that Satan opposed him, bringing an accusation against him
relative to the murder of the Egyptian; in consequence of
which he was unworthy of such an honorable burial" (*Lange's
Commentary*).

Because Moses and Elijah were seen talking with our Lord
on the Mount of Transfiguration (Luke 9:30), some students
have inferred that Moses was at some time previously res-
urrected. Wrote Fausset: "Buried by Jehovah in a valley
in Moab over against Beth-peor, Moses was probably translated soon after, for he afterward appears with the translated
Elijah and Jesus at the transfiguration . . . His sepulcher
therefore could not be found by man" (*Bible Cyclopedia*).

One other passage may be said to lend some support to
such an inference. The archangel is associated with future
resurrection in I Thessalonians 4:16; therefore he may have
been associated with the assumed translation of Moses' body
in the past.

If so, it is conceivable that the contest between Michael
and Satan could have taken place at that time. However,
such a resurrection or translation of Moses' body is entirely
without scriptural support, while his burial has been made
the subject of clear revelation.

Lending some support to the probable and more widely
held explanation is the fact that the Israelites actually did,
later, pay idolatrous worship to the brazen serpent Moses
had made (II Kings 18:4).

Even though God's Word were devoid of any light whatsoever on the angelic contest to which Jude refers, the example of Michael, the chief prince of God's hosts, should be taken as a terrible warning against evil speaking. Attacking God's people, speaking or writing accusations against institutions which honor the Lord and are honored by Him, are acts which bear the marks of a falling away from the teaching of the Bible rather than of subjection to it.

A discerning Christian, well taught in the Word, will view with sorrow the spectacle of one believer attacking another. What bitterness and strife, what malice and envy are revealed as present in the human heart when a man thus disobeys the Scripture which might have kept him from sinning against the Lord! Satan's power to deceive is nowhere more graphically demonstrated than when one man judges another, thinking that he is thereby furthering the work of God in the world. Contending for the faith is one thing; being contentious is another. The one we are commanded to do; the second we are commanded to avoid (Titus 3:9).

Michael the archangel dared not bring against the Devil a railing judgment, but said, "The Lord rebuke thee." In the mouth of two witnesses every word shall be established. We are given in Zechariah 3:2 a picture of the Lord Himself referring the responsibility of judgment to Jehovah. He said to Satan: "The Lord rebuke thee, O Satan; even the Lord that hath chosen Jerusalem rebuke thee: is not this a brand plucked out of the fire?" The judgment of God is according to truth; the judgment of men is not.

It is instructive to observe that Michael's words concerning Satan were restricted to his adversary alone. An accusation brought by one man against his fellow might not be so serious if it were a matter of man to man, but when it is publicized, no one can tell how far it will go, how twisted it will become, or what harm it will ultimately do.

LIKE CREATURES WITHOUT REASON

But these rail at whatsoever things they know not: and what they understand naturally, like the creatures without reason, in these things are they destroyed (v. 10).

WITH VERSE 10 before us, we are reminded that the one thought linking verses 8, 9, and 10 together is this same railing at dignities, against which Michael's example stands as a warning. The archangel, although dealing with Satan himself, and possessing a more perfect knowledge than ours, dared not to speak in judgment. "But these rail at whatsoever things they know not." An apostate does not hesitate to speak out in condemnation concerning matters about which he does not know enough to make him a judge over others.

This word "rail" comes from a Greek root that has given us our word "blaspheme" by transliteration. It means "to speak reproachfully," "to calumniate." We must not forget that Jude 10 is not written primarily about atheists, who revile our holy faith in total blindness to the truth (II Cor. 4:3, 4), nor is it written about the saints themselves, but rather about those who once had a knowledge of the truth and afterward fell away. It is not surprising that an atheist or an apostate should reproach the Lord's people, but it is an amazing spectacle when any part of these terrible verses is found to be illustrated among professing Christians who do not dream that they are exhibiting a mark of the very apostasy which they abhor.

What are the "things they know not," against which apostates rail? Some of them are mentioned in Revelation 13:6, where the same word appears in connection with the beast, who "opened his mouth in blasphemy against God, to blaspheme his name, and his tabernacle, and them that dwell in heaven." The word appears also in I Peter 3:16: "They speak evil of you."

It is a solemn thing to hear or to read statements of this sort being made in our day by men who abide not in the truth, and to realize that these are some of the men of whom Jude wrote. We know their destiny, awful though it is to contemplate. Although they are able to deceive some who listen to their pernicious words, they do not know whereof they speak. They are blind leaders of the blind. God permits them for the present to "speak evil of the things they understand not" (II Peter 2:12), but He reveals that they will finally be taken and destroyed.

There is a realm which these men "understand naturally, like the creatures without reason." It is the realm of the natural world, of which the unreasoning beasts likewise have knowledge. Two different words for "knowing" appear in verse 10. The first, *oida,* refers to deeper knowledge, and the second, *epistao,* refers to perception by the animal senses and faculties. Apostates have no deeper knowledge, but they do have superficial understanding.

The Holy Spirit has here also chosen the lowest word that is used of men in Scripture, *physikos,* when He refers to these as *natural* men. An apostate is a fleshly man possessing no higher life of the Spirit. Even though he may be looked upon as having a form of godliness, his lower nature dominates him. He is "of the world." While scorning true believers as "other worldly," he interests himself in the things of this present life. His highest religious thinking has to do with social reform and alleviating human suffering through natural means. He cares not for the souls of those who perish.

It will be noticed that verse 10 presents the three marks of apostasy in reverse order from the way they were set forth in verse 8. There is railing, there is limitation to natural understanding because that dominion which would have called to the higher knowledge of the things of the Spirit has been despised, and there is the closing phrase of verse 10, "in these things they are corrupted" (the marginal rendering, which also follows the King James Version).

In verse 8 the word *defile* has the meaning "to dye" or "to stain," and it speaks of contamination. But in verse 10, the word rendered "corrupted" means "spoiled" or "ruined," and pictures the utter destruction which finally results from the stain of sin. It is therefore rendered "destroyed" in our text. The same word appears in Ephesians 4:22: "The old man, which is *corrupt* according to the deceitful lusts." That is, the natural man is utterly ruined in God's sight. He must become a new creature before God can bring him to Heaven.

An apostate is therefore represented in verse 10 as one who rails at the truth, limits himself for this present life to mere natural knowledge, and finally perishes eternally in his own corruption. Thus, there is an acceleration downward for those who embark upon the course of apostasy. Verse 11 will be seen to bring forth this truth in startling clarity.

THREE MEN FROM THE PAST

Woe unto them! for they went in the way of Cain, and ran riotously in the error of Balaam for hire, and perished in the gainsaying of Korah (v. 11).

THE TREMENDOUS SWEEP of the revelation in Jude 11 is almost beyond comprehension. Here is a declaration of woe unto those guilty of apostasy, woe issuing from a three-fold sin into which they have entered by reason of their falling away from the path of subjection to the Lord Jesus Christ. Each phrase is sufficiently profound to warrant most careful study; each word is pregnant with meaning.

This is not surprising, because verse 11 is the heart of the epistle's structure. It stands midway between illustrations drawn from the supernatural realm (v. 9) and from the world of Nature (vv. 12, 13). It is preceded by apostasy in history; it is followed by apostasy in prophecy. It makes personal through individual examples the sinfulness of sins already set forth in corporate examples.

Observe first of all the characters who are here introduced into this divine summary of the acts of the apostates, in preparation for the final prophetic book of the Bible, the Revelation. Cain was a tiller of the soil; Balaam was a prophet; Korah was a prince in Israel. One reason for this selection of three men may be to demonstrate that apostasy is not confined to one class of persons. This evil is not peculiar to religious leaders. It touches prophets, princes, and people alike. There are apostates in pulpit, palace, and poorhouse. Individually Cain, Balaam, and Korah speak of particular aspects of what it means to fall away from the truth; together they present a complete picture.

Notice also a remarkable progress of thought in our text. Apostates first enter upon a wrong path; they then run riotously down that path; finally they perish at its end. Apostasy moves at an ever-accelerating pace on a road which runs downhill. In the passage before us there is no suggestion of a halt or a turning back from the way which leads to destruction. No hope for apostates is to be found in all of Jude. Their doom is sure. To them is reserved the blackness of darkness forever.

The hopelessness of the picture reminds us of Hebrews 6:4-6: "It is impossible for those who were once enlightened, and have tasted of the heavenly gift, and were made partakers of the Holy Ghost, and have tasted the good word of God, and the powers of the world to come, if they shall fall away, to renew them again unto repentance."

Like the swine of II Peter 2:20-22, such were never the true sheep of the Good Shepherd. Like the swine of Mark 5:13, the whole herd of apostates run violently down a steep place into the sea of God's wrath, called in Scripture the lake of fire. Once they come under the power of "doctrines of demons" (I Tim. 4:1) so that they fall away consciously from the truth of God they once tasted, there seems to be no arresting their downward course. How else can the terrible words of our blessed Lord be explained, "They could not believe" (John 12:39)? What other explanation unfolds the meaning of II Thessalonians 2:10-12: "They received not the love of the truth, that they might be saved. And for this cause God sendeth them a working of error, that they should believe a lie: that they all might be judged who believed not the truth, but had pleasure in unrighteousness"?

Read the text again. It is an inspired commentary on the peril of turning away from the truth of John 14:6. Christ is the Way, the Truth, the Life. An apostate is one who will not have the Son of man to reign over him. He knowingly chooses the way of Cain for the way of Christ, the error of Balaam for the truth of Christ, the perishing of Korah for the life of Christ.

Another element in the progress of thought in Jude 11 appears if we translate it more literally. "In the way of Cain they went away, and in the wandering of Balaam for reward they rushed headlong, and in the rebellion of Korah they perished." Apostasy begins with a way, it leads to a wandering, it becomes a rebellion. Men enter that false way, they rush headlong in that wandering, they perish in that rebellion.

It is necessary to recall some of the details in each of three Old Testament records if we are to understand what these three examples signify. What is the way of Cain? In Psalm 1, it is called the way of sinners, the way of the ungodly. Solomon referred to it when he wrote: "There is a way that seemeth right unto a man, but the end thereof are the ways of death" (Prov. 16:25). The Bible often makes reference to it.

Genesis 4:1-7 informs us that Cain brought a sacrifice to God of the fruit of the cursed ground, while Abel brought a lamb of the flock. We know both boys had been taught the truth that God could be approached only through the blood of an innocent substitute, because we know that Abel brought his lamb "by faith" (Heb. 11:4), that is, by believing what God had said about it. Cain brought something else; doubtless aesthetically more pleasing than a slain lamb, but displeasing to God because it meant the setting aside of His word. This is the first reference to the way of Cain.

When the Bible doctrine of the shed blood is set aside for something else, so that a preacher offers some message other than the good news of salvation from sin through Christ, he walks in the way of Cain. He may not become a murderer as did Cain, but he has taken Cain's place of rejection of God's way of salvation. He may not think he

is defiled with the blood of his brother, but he has taken
Cain's place in spurning God's gracious offer of salvation
through the shedding of blood, apart from which there is
no remission (Heb. 9:22). If he teaches others by precept
or example to follow his pernicious way, he actually becomes
guilty of their blood. "When I say unto the wicked, Thou
shalt surely die; and thou givest him not warning, nor
speakest to warn the wicked from his wicked way, to save
his life; the same wicked man shall die in his iniquity; but
his blood will I require at thine hand" (Ezek. 3:18).

The most arresting contrast between the two paths to be
found in all Scripture was given by Christ in Matthew 7:
13, 14: "Broad is the way that leadeth to destruction . . .
narrow is the way which leadeth unto life." He spoke of two
ways, two gates, two companies and two destinies which
have ever divided humankind. Few there be that find the
narrow way; many there be that go on the broad way.

The men of whom Jude writes "went away" (lit.) in this
wrong path. The word means to pass from one place to
another, to depart. The same original term appears in Matthew 25:41: *"Depart* from me, ye cursed, into everlasting
fire, prepared for the devil and his angels."

Jude is speaking of those who once were enlightened by
the truth concerning Christ and convicted by it. They vol-
untarily departed from their position and cast away their
opportunity. In another day they will be compelled to depart from Christ forever. The free choice of the present
determines the unchangeable destiny of the future.

Further to describe those who have entered upon the way
of Cain, the Holy Spirit now changes the figure from Cain
to Balaam, and introduces new terminology. Riotously they
live before they perish. They are lovers of pleasures more
than lovers of God (II Tim. 3:4). The expression "ran
riotously" is even more graphic in the original Greek. They
"have been poured forth," like a reservoir bursting its banks
and running on a rampage. When the restraint of Christ is

thrown aside, there is little to check the evil inclinations of the corrupt human will.

It will be remembered that Balaam was a prophet greedy for gold. As Israel came to the end of her wilderness wanderings and was about to enter the Promised Land, the chief men of the idolatrous nations Moab and Midian, fearing Israel, sought to hire Balaam to curse that nation. When the prophet sought counsel from the Lord, He said: "Thou shalt not go with them; thou shalt not curse the people: for they are blessed" (Num. 22:12). Not satisfied with this answer, which should have been sufficient had he honored the word of God, Balaam made further request to go, and was given permission, only to discover that God would not allow him to utter anything but blessings upon Israel.

As Moses summarized it: "They hired against thee Balaam the son of Beor of Pethor of Mesopotamia, to curse thee. Nevertheless the Lord thy God would not hearken unto Balaam; but the Lord thy God turned the curse into a blessing unto thee, because the Lord thy God loved thee" (Deut. 23:4, 5).

Deprived of the rewards promised him by Balak, king of Moab, Balaam's covetous heart conceived an evil thought. If he could counsel the women of Midian and Moab to tempt the Israelites and cause them to sin, God would have to punish His people, Balak's purpose would be served, and Balaam would be rich.

Three brief quotations must suffice to describe the success of this plan to circumvent the Lord's purpose. The daughters of Moab and Midian seduced the sons of Israel. They "called the people unto the sacrifices of their gods: and the people did eat, and bowed down to their gods. And Israel joined himself unto Baal-peor: and the anger of the Lord was kindled against Israel" (Num. 25:2, 3). How this came about is recorded in Numbers 31:16: "Behold, these [women of Midian] caused the children of Israel, through the counsel of Balaam, to commit trespass against the Lord in the matter of Peor, and there was a plague among the congregation of the Lord."

To these statements may be added Revelation 2:14: "The doctrine of Balaam, who taught Balak to cast a stumbling block before the children of Israel, to eat things sacrificed to idols, and to commit fornication."

Balaam took the way of Cain. He doubtless lived riotously afterward, but he perished miserably with the enemies of God at last. The inevitable day of judgment finally came for him. Israel overcame her enemies, and "Balaam also the son of Beor, the soothsayer, did the children of Israel slay with the sword among them that were slain by them" (Josh. 13:22). He perished at the end of the broad way.

These old records tell us what Jude means by "the error of Balaam for hire." It is the error of all apostates, the sacrificing of eternal riches for temporal gain. It is running riot on the broad ways of earth. It is lust for "the pleasures of sin for a season," greed for "the treasures of Egypt" (Heb. 11:25). It is a compelling desire to gain some part of the world even at the loss of the soul. What does such an error profit a man (Mark 8:36)? Many have followed the example of Demas by forsaking God's people, "having loved this present world" (II Tim. 4:10).

Once more the Holy Spirit introduces an Old Testament character through Jude, to complete this concise description of apostasy found in three men who fell away from revealed truth. Apostates perish in the "gainsaying," or rebellion, of Korah.

The student of Scripture should not overlook the fact that all three statements in Jude 11 are in the past tense. It is a very solemn truth that in God's sight those who go on in the way of Cain have *already* perished. The doom of apostates is no less sure than the glorification of the saints as set forth in Romans 8:30: "Whom he called, them he also justified: and whom he justified, them he also glorified." God speaks of both the doom of the apostate and the hope of the Christian as being in the past tense; He "calleth those things which be not as though they were" (Rom. 4:17).

"Gainsaying" in the Greek text is *antilogia,* meaning "against the word." This suggests a further example of downward progress in our text. Cain ignored the word revealed to himself and to Abel; Balaam subtly opposed the word which had been spoken; Korah appeared in open rebellion against the Word of God.

Korah was a Levite, cousin to Moses (Exod. 6:18-21). Under his leadership and that of his associates, Dathan and Abiram, a rebellion against the authority of Moses and Aaron was begun. It reached its crisis when "the ground clave asunder that was under them, and the earth opened her mouth, and swallowed them up, and their houses, and all the men that appertained unto Korah, and all their goods. They, and all that appertained unto them, went down alive into the pit, and the earth closed upon them: and they perished from among the congregation" (Num. 16:31-33).

What was the great sin which sent Korah to the pit? He had rejected the mediator whom God had appointed to stand between Himself and His people. He spoke evil of dignities chosen of God. In rebelling against Moses and Aaron, he was rejecting, in type, Christ the one Mediator (cf. Heb. 3). Therefore, he became in one terrible moment of judgment the figure of all who rebel against the Word and reject God's offer of salvation. His destiny became the pit.

Korah had dared to think "all the congregation are holy" (Num. 16:3), and to presume that he could approach a holy God without the required mediator. It is not necessary to draw the parallel today with those who teach that all men are sons of God, that mankind can come to God another way than through Christ crucified and risen.

"Woe unto thee!" said our Lord to apostates in His day after they had turned away from Him (Luke 10:13). "Woe unto them!" writes the Spirit through Jude of all who fol-

low them into the way of Cain, upon which so many have
been wandering and perishing ever since the dawn of history. God grant that we shall be given discernment to recognize such men in our day, and grace to stand against
them, earnestly contending for our most holy faith.

FIVE WORD-PICTURES

These are they who are hidden rocks in your love-feasts when they feast with you, shepherds that without fear feed themselves; clouds without water, carried along by winds; autumn trees without fruit, twice dead, plucked up by the roots; wild waves of the sea, foaming out their own shame; wandering stars, for whom the blackness of darkness hath been reserved forever (vv. 12, 13).

THE MORE MINUTELY we examine this great epistle, the more impressive becomes its delineation of the doctrine of apostasy. Jude has now covered the whole creation, from angels to men and brute beasts. There yet remains the realm of nature, and in five flashing inspired word-pictures he brings before us the earth, the air, the trees, the sea, and the starry heavens, to complete the panorama needed to provide the Church with a magnificent final summary of conditions as they are to be in Christendom just before the scenes of Revelation are unveiled.

Five natural phenomena provide instructive pictures of the true nature of apostasy. Before looking at them separately, it is instructive to look at them together, since they have been selected and assembled in a definite order by the Spirit of God. Because they represent new truth, they do not duplicate the teaching of the Old Testament records to which Jude is an index. There is no emphasis in them of a defiling of the flesh, a despising of dominion, or a deriding of dignities. Neither do they speak in particular of a way, an error, or a gainsaying.

Instead, five other characteristics of apostasy are illustrated. Hidden rocks tell of its unseen danger; waterless clouds, its false promise; autumnal trees, its barren profession; raging waves, its wasted effort; wandering stars, its aimless course. In the same order are five statements suggesting the selfishness, the helplessness, the fruitlessness, the shamefulness, and the hopelessness of apostates.

In reading this list, one is reminded by way of contrast with the Lord whom these men deny. He is the Rock of our salvation; they are hidden rocks threatening shipwreck to the faith. He comes with clouds to refresh His people forever; these are clouds which do not even bring temporary blessing. He is a tree of life; these are trees of death. He leads beside still waters; these are like the restless troubled sea. He is the bright and morning Star, heralding the coming day; these are wandering stars presaging a night of eternal darkness.

Hidden rocks. The word describes a ledge or reef of rock reaching up from the earth below the surface of the ocean to threaten anything which may come in contact with it. The appropriateness of the term becomes impressive when we reflect upon what at first appears to be a mixed metaphor. Hidden rocks in the love-feasts of Christians—is this not a strange expression? Not when we realize that these rocks brought shipwreck to the love-feasts of the early Church!

The custom of holding such feasts has been gone for centuries. It was already foundering in Paul's day. At the time he wrote I Corinthians 11:21 believers had established the practice of meeting together for a meal called the *agape,* or love-feast, preceding the observance of the Lord's Supper. Wealthier believers supplied the need of poorer folk. All shared alike in a demonstration of the love which bound together all members of the family of God. Then some began to come to these gatherings who thought only of themselves. They ate their own delicacies in the presence of others who were hungry. They even became drunken, so that Paul had to write and rebuke them.

Jude recognizes this selfishness as a manifestation of apostasy. All who came to the love-feasts were originally professing believers, or they would not have come, nor would they have been accepted. But when some began to "pasture" or feed themselves, enjoying their abundance while others about them had nothing, they revealed that they did not belong in the heavenly atmosphere of the saints. They were giving evidence of a falling away from the truth they had once claimed to embrace.

Clouds without water. This is the opposite to what is found in Luke 12:54: "When ye see a cloud rise out of the west, straightway ye say, There cometh a shower, and so it is." The clouds of which Jude writes give promise of refreshing rain for the thirsty desert of the world of the lost, but they bring nothing except disappointment. Solomon wrote of them long before: "Whoso boasteth himself of a false gift is like clouds and wind without rain" (Prov. 25:14). False is their profession. They have never accepted the gift of God and its living water (John 4:10).

Clouds without water not only deceive and discourage those who are thirsting for the water of life, and might drink if they could; they carry the threat of storm to the Christian. They darken his skies, tend to dim his vision of the Sun of Righteousness, but they must finally pass away (Hosea 13:3).

The same word here rendered "without water" is used in Matthew 12:43 of the "dry places" in which evil spirits are said to wander. Taken together, the two passages suggest a connection between apostates and unseen evil spirits who influence or control them. The suggestion is strengthened by what follows.

These clouds without water are "carried aside by winds." Beyond the simplicity of the words the instructed believer may detect the invisible influence of wicked spirits, for the

word for "wind" and the word for "spirit" are identical in
the Old Testament (*ruach*), and the New Testament word
for spirit (*pneuma*) is also used of the wind (John 3:8).
The actual helplessness of these men is indicated here. Without realizing it, they are bondslaves to Satan and his hosts.
"To whom ye yield yourselves servants to obey, his bondslaves ye are" (Rom. 6:16, marg.).

Although unstable Christians may be carried *about* by
every wind of doctrine (Eph. 4:14), true Christians are
never said to be carried *aside* by the winds of the prince of
the power of the air, as these men are. A cloud cannot
go where it pleases, but must go where the winds carry it.
Invisible influences are responsible for the direction in which
men without Christ are drifting.

A refreshing contrast appears in II Peter 1:21. God's
prophets spake as they were borne along by the Holy Spirit.
What they wrote is the very dew of Heaven distilled for the
Lord's own. The same Holy Spirit bears along the faithful
expositor of Scripture as he proclaims the inspired message
of Heaven to men. "As cold waters to a thirsty soul, so
is good news from a far country" (Prov. 25:25).

Autumn trees. The Greek term is formed of the word
for "autumn," the season for fruit, and the word "to wane."
Is this not a clear suggestion, if rendered literally, "late
autumn trees," of the fact that the great apostasy is to come
as the autumn of the Church Age is waning and the winter
of judgment is nigh? The harvest of the earth will one day
be ripe. God will thrust in His sickle. The storms of His
wrath will burst upon the earth. But before this, He will
gather His wheat, all true believers, into His barn (Matt.
13:30).

This description ought to be read in the light of a state-
ment made by our Lord: "Every plant, which my heavenly
Father hath not planted, shall be rooted up" (Matt. 15:13).
He was speaking of the Pharisees, who were offended by
His words. That is, Christ announced that men who did not

accept His teaching would be rooted up some day, like undesirable plants. This was in keeping with Old Testament prophecy: "The wicked shall be cut off from the earth, and the transgressors shall be rooted out of it" (Prov. 2:22).

Those who honor the law of the Lord are likened in Psalm 1 to trees planted by rivers of water, who bring forth their fruit in their season. Just as Psalm 1:3 speaks in one phrase of a tree, and in the next of the person whom the tree represents, so Jude 12 speaks of the ungodly as trees, but uses terminology also which has its primary application to the men of whom the trees speak. They are twice dead. Some commentators have puzzled over the question of how a *tree* can be twice dead, concluding that the expression refers to the apparent death of the late autumn, and the real death of uprooting. It is simpler to permit Jude the freedom found in Psalm 1.

"Twice dead" stands between "without fruit" and "rooted up." Apostates are dead to the fruit of profession and dead to the root of possession. Their fruitlessness now is a sign of death in life. "She that liveth in pleasure is dead while she liveth" (I Tim. 5:6). Their uprooting will be their second death, when Matthew 15:13 and Proverbs 2:22 are fulfilled. Their doom is already sealed. In the sight of God they are already uprooted and cast into the lake of fire.

Believers, on the contrary, are fruitful in every good work, because they are rooted and grounded in Christ. "Blessed is the man that trusteth in the Lord. . . . He shall be as a tree planted by the waters, and that spreadeth out her roots by the river, and shall not see when heat cometh, but her leaf shall be green; and shall not be careful in the year of drought, neither shall cease from yielding fruit" (Jer. 17:7, 8).

Wild waves. The sea is used more than once in the Bible as a symbol of those who do not know God. "The wicked are like the troubled sea, when it cannot rest, whose waters cast up mire and dirt. There is no peace, saith my God, to

the wicked" (Isa. 57:20, 21). Isaiah wrote of troubled
waves and their action of littering the white beaches of the
old creation, reminding us of the troubled minds of the
ungodly which cause their lips to cast up all manner of
evil-speaking against the saints of the Most High in His new
creation.

Jude wrote of the uncontrolled wildness of the waves of
men who have apostatized from the truth, revealing their
own shamefulness and helplessness as they vainly foam
against men who stand firmly upon the Rock. God has imposed a limit beyond which the sea cannot go (Ps. 104:9).
He has given the promise to His own: "Nothing shall by
any means hurt you" (Luke 10:19). Every evil thing spoken
or done against us will finally issue in glory to God "in the
day of visitation" (I Peter 2:12).

Like the other vivid figures used by Jude, this one is part
of a complete Bible word-picture. Wrote the psalmist of
our Lord: "Thou rulest the raging of the sea: when the
waves thereof arise, thou stillest them" (Ps. 89:9). All
power belongs to Him. Just as Christ stilled the storm on
Galilee, so He will some day be pleased to still these wild
waves of the sea of lost humanity. It will again be by the
word of His power.

Until then, the wild waves will continue to rage, even
though they never do any more than foam out their own
shame. When the waves and billows swept over Christ and
the floods of ungodly men overflowed Him (Ps. 18:4; 42:7),
He was revealed as Victor over them after they had receded.
The powers of darkness were certain of triumph. Had the
princes of this world known that Calvary would mean their
own defeat, "they would not have crucified the Lord of
glory" (I Cor. 2:8).

Waves throw themselves against every rocky barrier
which may stand in their way, but anyone who has watched
the sea knows how ineffectual the waves are. The barrier
still stands as the waves subside into foam. Often through-

out the history of the Christian Church there has come what seemed to be a tidal wave of destructive power against it, but each successive onslaught has died in the presence of a Church still standing and sending forth its light over the troubled sea. The Church will continue to stand when all raging waves have cast themselves against its truth for the last time, and the Scripture is fulfilled, "there was no more sea" (Rev. 21:1).

Wandering stars. Our world is one of a family of planets revolving around the sun, lighted by the sun, and controlled by the sun. Sometimes a wandering body from outer space is seen entering the atmosphere, flashing brilliantly for a moment, then either dashing onward in its erratic course into outer space again, or becoming a dark cinder through friction with the air. We call them "shooting stars." Jude uses them as striking examples of apostasy.

An apostate is one who comes under the illuminating influence of the Sun of righteousness (Mal. 4:2), believes "for a time" in the One who was called the Light of the world, then falls away without ever having become one of the family whose center is the Son of God. "Everyone that doeth evil hateth the light, neither cometh to the light, lest his deeds should be reproved" (John 3:20). "The stars in their courses" (Judg. 5:20) and the planets in the solar system move in orbits ordained for them by their Creator, whereas a wandering star is not subject to God's governmental control, and so its destiny is outer darkness.

A cursory reading of Jude might give the impression that a contradiction exists between the eternal fire of verse 7 and the eternal darkness of verse 13. A comparison with other Scriptures resolves the difficulty. Darkness designates the place of torment, while fire describes its nature. In II Thessalonians 1:6-10 the wicked are said to be judged in flaming fire and punished with everlasting destruction from the presence of the Lord who is light.

Two elements are found in the judgment awaiting all

apostates. Fire is evidently the only word in human language which can suggest the anguish of perdition. It is the only word in the parable of the wheat and the tares which our Lord did not interpret (Matt. 13:36-43). He said: "The field is the world," "the enemy . . . is the devil," "the harvest is the end of the world," "the reapers are the angels." But we look in vain for such a statement as, "the fire is . . . " The only reasonable explanation is that fire is not a symbol. It perfectly describes the reality of the eternal burnings.

"The blackness of darkness forever" is equivalent to everlasting destruction from the presence of the Lord. He Himself said: "The children of the kingdom shall be cast out into outer darkness: there shall be weeping and gnashing of teeth" (Matt. 8:12). In His presence is fullness of joy (Ps. 16:11). Who can conceive an eternity out of His presence, in the unending blackness of darkness, where no other creature can be seen, where no ray of light ever penetrates, where those who spurned God's offer of love forever wander without hope, alone and lost? Such is the picture drawn by Jesus and by Jude.

Reviewing these five illustrations from the realm of nature, we notice that they present the same terrible picture of downward progress found earlier in the epistle. In verses 5-7 we read of the end of earthly life, of being reserved for future judgment, and of the vengeance of eternal fire. Verse 11 pictures an entering upon a way, a downward plunge, a final perishing. The passage now before us begins with men who are present at a love-feast of Christians. Next they are carried away, then they are represented as fruitless, uprooted, dead. After death their shame is mentioned, with outer darkness as their final destiny.

By way of contrast, true believers enjoy a lifelong love-feast. They are borne along by the Holy Spirit, unmoved by winds of false doctrine. After a life of fruitfulness, they go home to be with Christ, in glory and honor. Forever afterward they dwell in light unutterable.

Instead of being lifeless, dangerous rocks, they are living stones (I Peter 2:5). Rather than waterless clouds, they are sources of living water (John 7:38). Far from being dead trees, they are called "trees of righteousness, the planting of the Lord" (Isa. 61:3). In contrast with raging waves, their peace is like a river and their righteousness as the waves of the sea (Isa. 48:18). Whereas wandering stars have reserved for them the blackness of darkness forever, true believers shall shine as the stars forever and ever (Dan. 12:3).

PROPHECY BEFORE THE FLOOD

And to these also Enoch, the seventh from Adam, prophe-
sied, saying, Behold, the Lord came with ten thousands of
his holy ones, to execute judgment upon all, and to convict
all the ungodly of all their works of ungodliness which they
have ungodly wrought, and of all the hard things which un-
godly sinners have spoken against him (vv. 14, 15).

IF IT WERE NOT FOR JUDE, we would know practically
nothing about prophecy uttered before the Flood. Early in
the first book of the Bible it is recorded that there was a
great antediluvian civilization. We read of cities, cattle rais-
ing, fine arts, education, and manufacturing (Gen. 4:17-22).
We also know something of the wickedness of those days
(Gen. 6:5), but God did not give to His people a written
revelation of antediluvian prophecy until His Word was
almost completed.

Enoch was a prophet, the only one from the centuries
before the Flood whose words have been preserved for us.
While some scholars discourse learnedly on where Jude
might have gotten this information, and others scoff openly
at what he has written, reverent scholarship recognizes that
the verses before us put Jude into a class with Moses, Paul,
Peter, and other holy men of God who "spake as they were
moved by the Holy Spirit" (II Peter 1:21).

Moses went even farther back into the mists of antiquity,
and wrote the story of the creation. Paul named the magicians of Egypt of whom Moses left no written record
(II Tim. 3:8), and quoted a statement by Christ not found

in the Gospels (Acts 20:35). Peter informs us that Noah was "a preacher of righteousness" (II Peter 2:5), a fact of which we otherwise would be ignorant.

The existence of an apocryphal Book of Enoch, containing a prophecy similar to this one given by Jude, has led some students to the unwarranted assumption that Jude copied from the apocryphal work. The Book of Enoch is a patchwork of writings by various unknown persons at various unknown times. It contains fanciful and legendary material, some of it quite ridiculous. Those who love the Word of God and trust it implicitly need not fear that any attack upon Jude will succeed in showing that he took any part of his epistle from such a volume.

If, as some think, there was still extant in the first century a record of some sort preserved from antediluvian times, it is not reasonable to assume that while an unknown writer had access to it, Jude did not. Most believers are satisfied that this epistle is inspired of God, without being troubled as to how God communicated its details to His servant.

Enoch is designated as "seventh from Adam." The seven are listed in Genesis 5 as Adam, Seth, Enos, Cainan, Mahalaleel, Jared, and Enoch. Thus the antiquity of the prophecy is emphasized and its author is distinguished from another Enoch, a son of Cain (Gen. 4:17). It is a curious fact that whereas it is hard to find helpful comment on this great prophecy from before the Flood, a great deal of speculation has been written on the words, "seventh from Adam." Lange, for example, devotes 101 lines to the phrase, while giving only 65 lines to the entire message of Enoch. Lange takes the position that the first six generations of the human race, characterized by sin and death, and followed by a seventh generation exhibiting a godly life without death, foreshadow six world periods of sin and death, to be succeeded by a seventh age, the kingdom of God on earth.

Although the prophecy quoted by Jude is the most ancient announcement of future events known to have been uttered by man, there is something else which has come down to us from Enoch which may actually be older. It is the name given by the prophet to his son, and it appears also to be a prophecy. "Enoch lived sixty and five years, and begat Methuselah" (Gen. 5:21).

Some Bible dictionaries give the meaning of this name as "man of a dart," on the theory that it is made up of an unusual Hebrew root *math,* a man, and another uncommon root *shelak,* a dart. It is necessary to reject this uncertain derivation of the name as not only meaningless, but as not truly a Biblical explanation. The root *math* is never used in the Bible for a man, although fourteen other Hebrew words are so translated. The root *shelak* appears only six times, once of a dart, twice of a weapon, and three times of a sword.

A far better interpretation of the name Methuselah is that it means "when he is dead, it shall be sent," from the Hebrew root *muth,* "to die," and the verb *shalak,* "to send forth." *Muth* is the common Old Testament word translated hundreds of times by the word *die,* eight of these occurrences being in Genesis 5 where the name Methuselah appears. The other root, *shalak,* the common word for *send,* is used sixty times in the Old Testament when God is said to *send* judgment on the earth, from the plagues of Egypt to the famine, fire, and pestilence of the prophets.

Fausset's *Bible Cyclopedia* is representative of the works presenting this as the probable name of Enoch's son: "Methuselah: he dies and it [the Flood] is sent. A name given prophetically by Enoch. He died in the year of the Flood. It is suggestive that *death* enters into the name of the longest liver."

Favoring this position is the fact that it is based on Bible language. It is also meaningful, because when Methuselah died, judgment from God was actually sent, according to the chronology of Genesis 5 (tradition says that he died seven days before the Flood). It is reasonable that Enoch, being a prophet, should thus have announced the coming of the Flood (Gen. 18:17; Amos 3:7).

During that period of human history every name had meaning. "Adam called his wife's name Eve [life, or life-giver]; because she was the mother of all living" (Gen. 3:20). Cain means "acquired" (Gen. 4:4); Seth means "appointed" (Gen. 4:25). Some names are prophetic, as in Genesis 17:5, where Abram's name was changed to Abraham, "father of many nations," because that was to be his destiny.

The name given by Enoch to his son may therefore be regarded as a prophecy which underlines the importance of the words we find recorded by Jude. In fact, the meaning of the name *Methuselah* casts brilliant light upon the outstanding fact in the entire life of the antediluvian prophet, his walk with God.

> And Enoch lived sixty and five years, and begat Methuselah: And Enoch walked with God after he begat Methuselah three hundred years, and begat sons and daughters: And all the days of Enoch were three hundred sixty and five years: And Enoch walked with God: and he was not; for God took him (Gen. 5:21-24).

It is not said that Enoch walked with God until after he begat Methuselah. For the first sixty-five years of his life he was certainly a man of God, but then something happened which caused him to enter into such a close fellowship with the Lord as to make him a marked man for the rest of his life. A son was born into his home, and Enoch was given the amazing revelation from God that when this child should die, every living creature upon the earth would be destroyed by a universal flood.

The child was named Methuselah. As Enoch watched his son grow, he knew that every time this strange name was spoken, the terrible prophecy of God was repeated: "When he is dead, it shall be sent." The life of all men hung upon the life of this one baby, this one boy, this one man, Methuselah. Every year he lived brought the announced catastrophic judgment one year closer.

Here is the key to Enoch's walk with God. Of what value was earthly gain, earthly pleasure? It would all be gone under divine wrath ere long. He knew that the end of all things was at hand. And so "Enoch walked with God after he begat Methuselah." He possessed an incentive to godly living comparable with that which is placed before Christians today. We are repeatedly enjoined to walk with God, and we have been given the motive, among others, that the time is short. The world is under doom from God.

There is no doubt that the removal without dying of this man before the coming of the Flood foreshadows the removal without dying of those who will have been walking with God prior to the judgments prophesied to follow the end of the present age. Enoch was translated without seeing death "by faith," that is, by believing God (Heb. 11:5). That is all anyone needs to escape future judgment.

Enoch's godly walk did not mean turning away from a normal life on earth. During the time he lived in the presence of God, "he begat sons and daughters." It may be presumed that they were saved, but their generation did not heed the prophecy given through the patriarch. For 120 years before the fulfillment of the prophecy inherent in the name Methuselah, Noah went about as a preacher of righteousness amid the godlessness of his time, warning of the coming Flood. Yet no one paid any heed except his own three sons and their wives.

Not even the translation of Enoch turned men away from their sinfulness, so far as we know. The wickedness of man became great, the earth was filled with violence (Gen. 6:5, 12). Whatever solemn impressions had been made by the prophet's departure were soon forgotten.

It is noteworthy that Methuselah lived to be the oldest man in all the Bible (Gen. 5:27). His 969 years speak strongly of the grace and longsuffering of God. The word had been given that when he was gone, the Flood would

be sent. But God is not willing that any should perish (II
Peter 3:9). Therefore He extended the life of Enoch's son
to provide maximum opportunity for men to repent and
turn to God. The revealed reason for the prolonging of the
present age is that men may be saved (II Peter 3:8, 9, 15).

If all these astonishing things hinge upon a prophecy given
by Enoch in a single word, how important should we consider the long utterance of the same prophet recorded by
Jude! Enoch not only saw clearly the coming of God's judgment in the Flood; he also foretold and warned against the
judgment which will take place at the coming of the Lord.
One word only is preserved to us of what Enoch said about
the end of the antediluvian civilization, but what a dreadful
event that turned out to be! A lengthy statement is preserved
of what he said about the end of the present order of things,
a judgment so terrible that even the best instructed Christians
can only faintly comprehend what it is to be like.

Four notable facts are emphasized by Enoch's prophecy.

We know the Lord's coming is sure. Said Enoch, "Behold,
the Lord came!" Like other prophets, he was given a vision
of the future. The veil was taken away, and he saw this
far-off event so clearly that he was able to describe it as
though it were already past. God, "able even to subdue all
things unto himself" (Phil. 3:21), has on many occasions
transported His servants across thousands of years of history
so that they actually beheld distant events as spectators. At
the opposite end of the Bible from Enoch, John saw the
Lord come from Heaven, followed by celestial hosts (Rev.
19:11-14). Both prophets beheld the same coming.

Enoch looked at what was unveiled before his eyes, and
said, as if in astonishment at so grand a consummation,
"Behold, the Lord came!" The first prophecy ever given
through a man, like the last (Rev. 22:20), has to do, not
with Christ's first coming in grace to bring salvation, but
with His second coming in judgment. In giving this truth
to us, the Holy Spirit used the past tense, the historic tense
of prophecy, as He does elsewhere in the prophetic Scrip-

tures. Nothing can change the facts of history after they
have happened. Nor can anything prevent this future event
about which the Spirit has written. In God's sight it has
already taken place.

Some day men will echo Enoch's words and exclaim,
"The Lord came!" They will see that everything turned out
exactly as the prophets foretold. It is possible to have this
certain knowledge now. Multitudes have it. By believing
what God has said about present salvation, they find John
7:17 fulfilled in themselves. They know that all of the
Scriptures are from God. They enter into a supernatural
assurance that the Bible is true in those parts which describe
the future, just as it is true in those parts which describe
the experience of present salvation.

We know who will accompany the Lord. "He came with
his holy myriads" (lit.). A great host was with the Lord
when He came to give the law. Wrote Moses: "The Lord
came from Sinai, and rose up from Seir unto them; he
shined forth from mount Paran, and he came with ten
thousands of saints: from his right hand went a fiery law
for them" (Deut. 33:2). The very same coming witnessed
by Enoch is mentioned in Zechariah 14:5: "The Lord my
God shall come, and all the saints with thee."

Who are these saints, or holy ones, whom Enoch saw
coming with the Lord? It is clear that the "holy ones" to
whom Moses referred were angels (Acts 7:53; Gal. 3:19),
and "all the holy angels" are to be with Christ when He
returns (Matt. 25:31). But believers are also to appear with
Christ in glory when He comes "with all his saints" (Col.
3:4; I Thess. 3:13). Therefore, the "holy myriads" seen by
Enoch may be said to have included both the holy angels
and the redeemed people of earth.

Myriads are associated with Christ at the judgment in
other passages. In Revelation 19:14 "the armies which were
in heaven" are seen following Him at His coming. In Daniel
7:10 it is written that "a fiery stream issued and came forth
from before him: thousand thousands ministered unto him,

and ten thousand times ten thousand stood before him: the judgment was set, and the books were opened."

Such revelations ought to deepen our sense of responsibility to the One who will thus honor His people. Here is a tremendous incentive to live as those who will one day stand with the awful Judge of the universe. "Do ye not know that the saints shall judge the world? . . . Know ye not that we shall judge angels?" (I Cor. 6:2, 3). The saints, according to the New Testament, are not exceptionally holy persons, but are those who have been separated unto God by believing the Gospel.

We know the purpose of His coming. It is to execute judgment upon all. The Lord came once to bring salvation; He will come again to bring judgment (Heb. 9:26-28). Jude's word for judgment is *krisis*. Christ used the same term when He spoke of the judgment of Sodom (Luke 10:14). It is the word found in Hebrews 10:27, "A certain fearful looking for of judgment"; and in II Peter 3:7, "the day of judgment and perdition of ungodly men."

Our Lord declared plainly that no believer will ever come into judgment (*krisis,* John 5:24). We will appear before the judgment seat of Christ to render an accounting for our service and to receive rewards, but an entirely different word, *bema,* is used in these passages (Rom. 14:10; II Cor. 5:10). Prior to the *krisis,* Christians will have been translated from earth to meet their Lord (I Thess. 4:13-18).

It is interesting to note that the unknown writer of the apocryphal Book of Enoch revealed his ignorance of the truth by making Enoch say: "He comes with myriads of saints to execute judgment on them" (trans. by Dillman, quoted in *Lange's Commentary*). Jude knew better than this. His epistle does not contain the error that the Lord will come to visit judgment on His people.

Who will be judged? Enoch said simply "all," but the Holy Spirit has enlarged upon this in scores of passages throughout the Bible. "He cometh to judge the earth" (Ps. 96:13), including "all the nations" (Joel 3:12, A.S.V.;

Matt. 25:32), with their cities (Matt. 11:22; 12:41). Every
man, whether living or dead, will ultimately be judged (II
Tim. 4:1; II Thess. 1:7-9). Although ungodly men are primarily in view in Jude 15, the fallen angels of verse 6 will
also be judged at that great day, as will other evil angels
(Isa. 24:21) and demons (Matt. 8:29). One company of
fallen creatures after another is to be tried and condemned.

Who will be this judge of all the earth (Gen. 18:25)?
"The Father judgeth no man, but hath committed all judgment unto the Son" (John 5:22). What will be the basis for
His decisions? It will be "according to truth," "according
to . . . deeds," "according to my gospel" (Rom. 2:2, 6,
16).

We know the result of the Lord's coming. All the ungodly will be convicted of all their works of ungodliness
which they have ungodly wrought. There will be no appeal
from the decision of the supreme court of the universe.

Matthew 25:31-46 describes the judgment and conviction
of men living on the earth at the time "when the Son of man
shall come in his glory, and all the holy angels with him."
The sentence will be: "Depart from me, ye cursed, into
everlasting fire."

Revelation 20:11-15 describes the later judgment and conviction of the ungodly dead. God's books are to be opened,
the dead are to be judged "out of those things which were
written in the books, according to their works." Their sentence will be their being cast into the lake of fire.

The heavens and the earth are now "kept in store, reserved
unto fire against the day of judgment and perdition of ungodly men" (II Peter 3:7). The day of judgment is also the
day of perdition. Enoch announced the conviction of all such
ungodly men; the Holy Spirit unfolds the terrible meaning
of this conviction throughout the Bible.

Jude reveals that God takes notice not only of works of
ungodliness, but also of the manner in which they have been
wrought. There may be a suggestion here that ungodly deeds
are sometimes wrought unknowingly, but the thought behind

every deed is known to God. He knows when an ungodly deed is also ungodly wrought. The Lord looks upon the heart (I Sam. 16:7).

"Hard things which ungodly sinners have spoken against him" will come up before this bar of God. The Judge spoke of this also: "I say unto you, That every idle word which men shall speak, they shall give account thereof in the day of judgment" (Matt. 12:36). What will be the amazement of sinners at that day, when they learn that every word, spoken with apparent impunity against God while they lived their ungodly lives, was made a matter of record, and must be accounted for!

HOW TO RECOGNIZE AN APOSTATE

*These are murmurers, complainers, walking after their
lusts (and their mouth speaketh great swelling words),
showing respect of persons for the sake of advantage* (v. 16).

T HE CHURCH will be without excuse if it fails to recognize
apostates when they appear. Over and over again Jude
uses the plainest of language to describe them. What are they
like? "These . . . defile the flesh," "these rail at whatsoever
things they know not," "these . . . are hidden rocks,"
"these . . . [are] ungodly," "these are murmurers," "these
are they who make separations." The inspired writer draws
portrait after portrait. He boldly writes a title beneath each
one, beginning with the word *these*, and clearly depicting
outstanding characteristics of apostates so that we shall know
them for what they are whenever we find them creeping in
among the saints.

Every generation since the days of the apostles has doubtless seen some of the marks given here, and speculated in its
literature on the question of whether conditions anticipated
in Jude had yet reached their final form. Succeeding generations, aware of what seems to them a deepening of the night,
wonder whether there could be a more grievous falling away
than that which they are witnessing.

Despite the terrible corruption of earlier periods of Church
history, some men of God in the twentieth century believe
they have more reason to think Jude's epistle is rapidly ap-
proaching complete fulfillment than others have had. Yet

who shall say that "the apostasy" is upon us? The language we are examining seems too strong to justify the identification of large numbers of individuals even in the second half of the twentieth century as unquestionably the people of whom these Scriptures speak. Granting that there is widespread apostasy, we must beware of setting dates for the return of Christ by suggesting that ours is the generation of which Jude wrote particularly.

Again three earmarks are set before us of the falling away which had begun in the early Church. Verse 16 contains three descriptive terms which bring to mind that which has gone before. These are murmurers, reminding us of the murmuring of the people of Israel. These are complainers, and we recall the angels' dissatisfaction with the place given to them by God. These are walking after their lusts, bringing to remembrance the inhabitants of Sodom and Gomorrah.

Although this trinity of wicked works is not new to our epistle, the language in which it is phrased is. The verse adds to the body of truth contributed by Jude to the subject of apostasy. The first word, *murmurers,* is found nowhere else in the New Testament. Nevertheless, its verb form does appear in such a way as to indicate why the Spirit chose it as an attribute of the pseudo Christianity of the last days.

In John 6:41 it is written: "The Jews then murmured at him, because he said, I am the bread which came down from heaven." They murmured, although He had revealed that they would never again hunger if they received Him. They murmured although He offered to them everlasting life. They murmured because He declared His deity. He claimed to have come down from Heaven, a fact accepted without question by true believers throughout the centuries, but a fact which apostasy cannot endure. These verses in John suggest that the primary application of Jude's word is not to any murmuring against Christians, but rather against Christ, although the meaning of the term is wide enough to include every form of the sin.

It is clear that a man can manifest apostasy in this way,

before he completes the evil trio by an outbreak of complaining and lustful living. When Jesus ended His discourse on the Bread of life, He "knew in himself that his disciples murmured" (John 6:61). "From that time many of his disciples went back, and walked no more with him" (John 6:66). To go back after hearing His words is apostasy. To walk no more with Him is to walk after one's lusts, to walk according to the course of this world (Eph. 2:2, 3). Such a walk, in John and in Jude, follows the sin of murmuring. Let us beware of the first, if we would avoid the guilt of the second!

Murmuring is therefore no sin of minor importance, no mere weakness of the flesh. It is one of the hallmarks of apostasy. Where it exists, there is the possibility that it reveals actual unbelief. Jude does not tell us what form of murmuring it is of which he writes, but Christ's use of the word establishes its meaning and authorizes us to understand that it includes murmuring against the Lord's own revelation of the nature of His being. It is the virtual denial of His deity. It is a latter-day fulfillment of Psalm 106:24-26: "They believed not his word: But murmured in their tents, and hearkened not unto the voice of the Lord. Therefore he lifted up his hand against them, to overthrow them." It is disobedience to I Corinthians 10:10: "Neither murmur ye, as some of them also murmured, and were destroyed of the destroyer."

Again Jude uses a term not found elsewhere in the New Testament, when he says that these are complainers. Here again we may turn to the Gospels for light upon our text. The verb form of Jude's word occurs in Mark 7:2, where the Pharisees "found fault." Their actual complaint is found in verse 5: "Why walk not thy disciples according to the tradition of the elders . . . ?" It brought forth one of the sternest rebukes our Lord ever administered: "Well hath Esaias prophesied of you hypocrites, as it is written, This people honoreth me with their lips, but their heart is far from me. . . . For laying aside the commandment of God, ye hold the tradition of men" (Mark 7:6, 8).

Whereas murmuring was directed against the Person of Christ, this fault-finding was directed against His followers. It is an arresting thought that fault-finding may mark a professing Christian as one who has turned his back upon the truth. Allowing for the weakness of the flesh which may cause faithful Christians sometimes to be overtaken with such a sin, we must recognize the possibility that complainers within a given church congregation may actually be apostates, who have laid aside the commandment of God as did the Pharisees. So often is this emphasized by Jude that we dare not ignore the evil importance of any attack upon Christ's disciples. "These . . . speak evil," wrote Jude in verse 8; "these speak evil," he said again in verse 10, and now he says, "these are murmurers, complainers." When a man opens his mouth to attack or accuse a true Christian, he may be one of Satan's ministers of righteousness (II Cor. 11:15). The apostle Paul warned believers not to keep company with any man who is a railer, even though he is called a brother (I Cor. 5:11).

It ought not to be overlooked that our Saviour's words in Mark 7 condemn the laying aside of the commandment of God in favor of the tradition of men. Making the Word of God of no effect through tradition is a form of apostasy, wherever it is found.

The literal meaning of the word *complainers* is sometimes given as "those who are dissatisfied with their lot." The fallen angels of verse 6 illustrate the term. They kept not their own principality, but left their proper habitation. Spiritual believers, careful to avoid the appearance of apostasy, will not complain about the station in life to which the Lord has called them. In whatsoever state they are in, therewith they will be content (Phil. 4:11). It is an interesting fact that those who murmur at what Christ said about His deity in our day are often those who also complain about, and seek to change, the social order in which they have been placed, the denominational confessions in which they have been reared, and the theological convictions of their fathers. They are dissatisfied with their own lot; they complain about others who stand faithful to the faith once for all delivered to the saints.

In the days of Moses, "When the people complained, it displeased the Lord: and the Lord heard it; and his anger was kindled; and the fire of the Lord burnt among them, and consumed them that were in the uttermost parts of the camp" (Num. 11:1). The Lord made it clear that He was displeased at the complaining described in Mark 7. Can there be any doubt about His displeasure when those who are known by His name find fault with their brethren today, in spite of both these passages, and in spite of Jude 16 as well?

For the third time we turn to the Gospels and find light upon our verse. Jude writes that these are "walking after their lusts." He uses the Greek word for lusts found upon the lips of Christ in the parable of the sower. "These are they which are sown among thorns; such as hear the word, And the cares of this world, and the deceitfulness of riches, and the lusts of other things entering in, choke the word, and it becometh unfruitful" (Mark 4:18, 19).

An apostate is one who has heard the Word, in measure has received it, then afterward has rejected it. It is of such that the Lord is speaking—men who permit the lusts of other things to choke the Word so that it does not bear fruit in them. It is of such also that Jude writes. The lusts of other things enter in after the good seed of the Word has been sown in their hearts: "All that is in the world, the lust of the flesh, and the lust of the eyes, and the pride of life" (I John 2:16). When this happens the Word is choked, the work of God in the life is arrested short of regeneration, and the walk becomes carnal, worldly, lustful. Apostasy has come, according to Mark, Jude, and Peter. In Mark lust is said to choke the Word, making it unfruitful. In Jude lust goes beyond this, and characterizes the walk. In Peter these who are "walking after their own lusts" (II Peter 3:3) openly become scoffers after rejecting the Word of God (II Peter 3:4, 5), and the cycle is complete.

Once more our trio of descriptive terms finds illustration in the Old Testament. Just as there were murmurers (Num. 14:2) and complainers (11:1) among the people who escaped from Egypt, so there were some who "fell a lusting" (11:4), a mixed multitude who had accompanied the Jews. They were with Israel but not of Israel. Like the men of whom Jude writes, they had crept in among God's people and turned the grace of God into lasciviousness. Thus we know such persons existed in Moses' day; they have been among the people of God throughout history; they are with us now. As we hear their murmuring and complaining, or have occasion to see something of their fleshly walk, let us take heed lest we partake of their sins.

There is another side to the character of these men: "Their mouth speaketh great swelling words." Anyone who has listened to the pompous utterances of a modern apostate religious leader needs little comment upon this passage of Scripture. Who has not heard or read great swelling words issuing from lips previously known for their denials of the eternal truths of the Word of God, great swelling words about how the Church or the social order or mankind in general could be helped by the adoption of what are essentially antichristian principles?

The context of II Peter 2:18, where the same expression is found, best interprets Jude's meaning. Those who give voice to great swelling words "have forsaken the right way, and are gone astray" (II Peter 2:15). The words are vain by which they seek to allure true Christians with promises of liberty, because they themselves are in bondage to corruption and lust (II Peter 2:19). Prating of freedom from the thralldom of Church creeds and the doctrines of historic Christianity, they actually try to bring God's people into slavery to doctrines of demons (I Tim. 4:1, marg.). Peter says they have known the way of righteousness, but afterward have turned from the holy commandment delivered unto them (II Peter 2:21). His terrible words should put any child of God on guard against such men, because they are like sick dogs. They are like sows wallowing in mud. They are unclean and vile in the sight of our holy God. Their great swelling words should be regarded as of no more value than the howling of a dog, or the squealing of a pig, as compared with the "form of sound words" found in the Bible which they have not found worthy of their attention.

These arrogant boasters have little respect for the Scripture of truth, but they are found "showing respect of persons for the sake of advantage." It is a striking fact that this phrase is associated with the other, in view of the common practice among men of the world of fawning upon each other with swelling words of adulation and praise in the expectation of gaining some advantage thereby. This sorry spectacle is witnessed upon the platform, when one man introduces another to an audience. It is seen in magazines and books, when "significant" speeches and writings are quoted as though they contained the distilled wisdom of the ages, for the sake of some advantage to be derived from flattery and adulation. When this practice invades the Church, believers have the right to think that the days of apostasy have come.

Doubtless there has always been some sacrifice of sincerity and truth in the effort to gain advantage through favoritism, but when it comes to be a frequent occurrence among religious leaders, dark days will be upon us. Professionalism will then have replaced the call of the Holy Spirit. Selfish gain through the flattery of princes of the Church will be sought by schemers desiring a certain pulpit, a coveted position of leadership, or a high salary.

From a careful study of these last two phrases of Jude 16, we may be certain that as the age of the Church draws to its close, two outstanding characteristics will follow the denial of the old faith. The occupants of many pulpits will be better known for swelling words about subjects foreign to the Gospel than for sober words about the glad tidings of salvation, and the selection of the occupants of these pulpits will be based upon methods giving advantage to flattery and favoritism more than methods which seek the mind of the Holy Spirit.

It is to be noted that these two evils are to originate not among faithful followers of Christ, but among the murmurers against Christ's deity, the complainers against His true disciples, the men who walk after their own lusts. Such men will encourage the use of swelling words in place of sound words; they will introduce policies which will make personal or ecclesiastical favor the criterion in the choice of leadership. Historically, this has followed the emergence of "lusts" within Christendom. It will be commonplace as the coming of Christ draws nigh.

REMEMBER THE WORD!

But ye, beloved, remember ye the words which have been spoken before by the apostles of our Lord Jesus Christ; that they said to you, In the last time there shall be mockers, walking after their own ungodly lusts. These are they who make separations, sensual, having not the Spirit (vv. 17-19).

WITH THESE VERSES the longest paragraph of Jude ends, in which he describes the men whose dark shadows will be athwart the church in the last days. He began it in verse 5 by putting us in remembrance of Old Testament Scriptures bearing upon the subject. He concludes it by asking us to remember something spoken by New Testament apostles concerning the great apostasy. A lengthy description of evil men is interrupted by an admonition to good men who are the beloved of the Lord.

After such a long dark word-picture the contrast is most striking. Light breaks forth suddenly as the Holy Spirit addresses the saints with a term of endearment. "But ye, beloved, remember ye the words!" Others may have forgotten the words spoken by God through Old Testament prophets and New Testament apostles; we cannot. We love to be reminded of them. Turning away from God's message is the mark of apostasy, but remembering and cherishing every word of God as pure and true (Prov. 30:5) is a mark of sonship. We therefore rejoice at His Word as those who find great spoil (Ps. 119:162). It is more to be desired than gold (Ps. 19:10).

We are asked to remember the *words* of the apostles. The doctrine of the inspiration of the very words of the Bible is set forth in Scripture as clearly and plainly as any other doctrine. Paul spoke "not in the words which man's wisdom teacheth, but which the Holy Ghost teacheth" (I Cor. 2:13). "The prophecy came not in old time by the will of man: but holy men of God spake as they were moved by the Holy Ghost" (II Peter 1:21). Without a doctrine of verbal inspiration, some creature of the dust might presume to think he could clothe the thoughts expressed in John 3:16 or in Psalm 23 with better language than now appears in the Bible!

Heeding Jude's admonition, we remember that in Acts 20:29 Paul warned against grievous wolves who would enter the church, "not sparing the flock." We recall I Timothy 4:1, (marg.): "In the latter times some shall depart from the faith, giving heed to seducing spirits, and doctrines of demons"; and II Timothy 3:1: "In the last days perilous times shall come," when men will manifest every evidence of apostasy found in Jude.

The most remarkable passage in the New Testament dealing with the specific subject of mockers in the end of the age is II Peter 3:1-3, which may be regarded as a divine commentary on Jude's statement. "Beloved . . . be mindful of the words which were spoken before by the holy prophets, and of the commandment of us the apostles of the Lord and Saviour: Knowing this first, that there shall come in the last days scoffers, walking after their own lusts."

The word translated "scoffers" in Peter and "mockers" in Jude is found nowhere else in the Bible. A mocker holds up to scorn the teaching of the Word of God. One such teaching particularly disliked is the promise that Christ will one day return to earth. They will say: "Where is the promise of his coming? for since the fathers fell asleep, all things continue as they were from the beginning of the creation." Peter reveals that this attitude is the result of willing ignorance.

The Word is heard and understood, and then by a deliberate act of the human will it is rejected and held in derision.

"Remember ye the words," admonishes Jude, and we recall that the New Testament is not alone in treating of the theme of verse 18. It is written in Proverbs 14:9, "Fools make a mock at sin," but the men of the latter days will nevertheless mock as they sin. In flouting what God has revealed they demonstrate that they are numbered among the fools of whom Solomon wrote. Progress in human wisdom and knowledge does not lessen the tendency of men to engage in ancient folly.

Another striking word-picture is found in the expression: "Walking after their own ungodly lusts." The same men who are likened to brute beasts in verse 10 are now said to be led about by lust, as an animal is led about with a ring in its nose. The animal walks obediently after its master; these walk after their ungodly lusts. Neither the captive bull nor the apostate enslaved by sin has any choice. He must go wherever he is led. He is in bondage. He may talk of liberty from traditional moral restraints, and despise the believer who lives a life of true holiness in the fear of God, but the apostate is himself a bondslave to corruption (II Peter 2:19).

Another of the threefold cords of divine truth found so frequently in Jude concludes the passage before us in verse 19. These men make separations, they are sensual, they have not the Spirit.

Once again we are faced with a word found nowhere else in the New Testament, rendered "they who make separations." Luther translated it, "those who make factions." It may be transliterated, "they who bring about divisions because of borderlines, or limits." Most students have understood this to refer to a drawing of boundary lines, or the establishing of ecclesiastical practices or regulations, within the church, by which factions are produced. It may be suggested rather that the reference is to limits which God has set up in His Word for the control of human conduct. Men sin when they overstep these divine limits. An apostate scoffs at the law of God, denies the authority of the Bible, lives outside the boundaries which true believers respect. In so doing, he causes divisions within the church.

When men of this sort multiplied early in the sixteenth century, the division they produced was so great that it led to the Reformation. Luther did not cause the division; it was caused by such men as are described by Jude, who had set aside the authority of God's Word. Church history reveals that many of the present divisions among Christians had their origin in similar circumstances. Without suggesting that this is by any means a major factor in the existence of many denominations within Christendom, we must recognize that it has been a factor. There comes to pass a neglect of the Scriptures, an emphasis upon something actually contrary to the teaching of the Bible, an overstepping of limits set forth in the Word of God, a protest by some who long for a return to Biblical principles, and finally a division.

The other side to this truth is given in I Corinthians 11:19: "For there must be also factions [Gr., heresies] among you, that they that are approved may be made manifest among you" (A.S.V.). Doctrines of demons have given rise to many false sects and divisions which bear the name of Christian, but apostasy has given rise to many divisions in which true believers have had to establish new churches and denominations in all good conscience, to preserve the truth of God in their generation. Apostates make separations; we cannot escape the truth of Jude 19. They may lay the blame on others who cannot endure their apostasy, but the Scriptures make it clear that they are themselves guilty. Jude will doubtless be proved a true prophet many times in the future, if the Lord does not return soon.

We need only turn back one page in our Bibles to find an illustration of Jude 19. Diotrephes is mentioned as a man who caused a division in the early church by refusing to

receive the apostle John (III John 9, 10). The reason was
that Diotrephes loved to have the pre-eminence, in which
he overstepped the Bible principle—"Let each esteem other
better than themselves" (Phil. 2:3). He set aside the teaching that Christ is to have the pre-eminence (Col. 1:18). This
man also manifested other characteristics of apostasy, speaking evil of John with malicious words, refusing to receive
the brethren, forbidding others who would have done so, and
even casting brethren out of the church. It is a significant
fact that the apostle John wrote in the verse immediately
after this description—"He that doeth evil hath not seen
God." Here was Diotrephes doing evil within the church.
He had not seen God nor beheld the Lamb of God. He was
evidently an apostate.

Jude next speaks of these men as sensual (Gr., *psychikos*).
The word does not mean lascivious (v. 4), nor walking in
ungodly lusts (v. 16), but rather, limited to the realm of
the senses, or dominated by the soul, the lower principle of
life. Man is a tripartite being consisting of spirit, soul, and
body (I Thess. 5:23). The spirit is the higher part of man,
giving him God-consciousness. The soul is the self, the per-
sonality, the seat of the emotions, and the will. The best
English equivalent of the word Jude uses is probably found
in I Corinthians 2:14, where it is rendered the *natural* man.

Believers are normally *spiritual,* if they are obedient to the
Word of God (I Cor. 2:15), although they may be *carnal,*
or babes in Christ (I Cor. 3:1). They are never said to be
sensual or natural men. Unsaved people, on the other hand,
are *natural* men, dominated by the senses or the self. They
receive not the things of the Spirit, thinking them to be
foolishness (I Cor. 2:14).

Therefore, when Jude reveals that the men of whom he
writes are sensual, or natural men, he is clearly stating once
more that apostates are people who have never become members of the family of God. There is no passage of Scripture
which could be made the basis for the concept that a natural

man ever was anything else but an unsaved man. An apostate is an individual who never became a child of God, no matter how deeply he may have been moved by the Gospel, no matter how public a profession he may have made, no matter how prominent the position he may have been given within the professing church. "These are they who are sensual," unsaved men.

We are now prepared more fully to understand Jude's concluding phrase in this description, "having not the Spirit." There can be no question but that this is a reference to the Holy Spirit of God. All men have a human spirit, darkened though it may be by sin. But all men do not have the Spirit of God. "If any man have not the Spirit of Christ, he is none of his" (Rom. 8:9).

If there were any remaining question about whether an apostate is a lost soul, or simply a Christian who is mistaken in some of his ideas, this certainly settles it. An apostate does not have the Holy Spirit. He is an unregenerate man. He lacks the distinguishing mark of the true believer, the Spirit who seals the transaction which takes place between an individual and his God in the moment of believing, seals it until the day of redemption (Eph. 1:13, 14).

A Christian is baptized by the Spirit into the Body of Christ, sealed by the Spirit, indwelt by the Spirit, taught by the Spirit, led by the Spirit. An apostate knows nothing of any of these things. Because we are sons, God hath sent forth the Spirit of His Son into our hearts, crying, Abba, Father (Gal. 4:6). Jude's words are among the most solemn in all the Bible. The man who heeds not the limits established in the Word of God to govern human life is a natural man who has not the Spirit. Unless he turns to Christ in sincere belief, he is forever lost.

BUILDING, PRAYING, LOOKING

But ye, beloved, building up yourselves on your most holy faith, praying in the Holy Spirit, keep yourselves in the love of God, looking for the mercy of our Lord Jesus Christ unto eternal life (vv. 20, 21).

THE MOCKERS described in verse 19 break down the work of God; the "beloved" of verse 20 build it up. Every word is in sharp contrast. Instead of ungodliness, separations, and sensuality we read of faith, love, and mercy. Prayer in the Spirit takes the place of an empty existence without the Spirit. The Triune God dominates the scene.

What does it mean to build up ourselves on our most holy faith? It is the counterpart of the truth set forth in verse 3, contending for the faith. Verse 3 is illustrated in the sword of Nehemiah 4:17, 18; verse 20 is the trowel. Weapons are supplied to us for our warfare; tools and materials are placed in our hands so that we may build for God. We must fight the enemy, but we must also construct a spiritual house that will please the Lord. Neither of these two admonitions of Jude can take precedence over the other without loss. If we contend without building, or if we build without contending, we are out of balance. We are giving heed to only a part of the Word of God.

Building in the Old Testament is mentioned many times, but it has reference to material things, from the first city erected in Genesis 4:17 to the last structure thrown down in Malachi 1:4. Hardly have we begun to read the New

Testament when we discover building of a different sort, in the spiritual realm. In Matthew 16:18 Christ speaks of building His Church. In Ephesians 2:20 we learn that we are "built upon the foundation of the apostles and prophets, Jesus Christ himself being the chief cornerstone." In I Peter 2:5 (A.S.V.) we read that we are "living stones . . . built up a spiritual house." It is further revealed in I Corinthians 3:10-15 that we by our works are building gold, silver, precious stones, or wood, hay, stubble, upon the foundation that is laid, which is Jesus Christ.

Jude writes of still another aspect of this many-sided truth. We are to build up ourselves, and the foundation is our most holy faith. Even though Christ is the Author and Finisher of our faith (Heb. 12:2), we have no right to say that Jude's exhortation is parallel to Paul's. His language and his meaning are both different.

Having already observed that II Peter and Jude throw light upon each other, we turn to II Peter 1:5-7 and discover a statement which teaches us much about the meaning of our passage. Peter also writes of a sort of building which has faith as its foundation. "Adding on your part all diligence, in your faith supply virtue; and in your virtue knowledge; and in your knowledge self-control; and in your self-control patience; and in your patience godliness; and in your godliness brotherly kindness; and in your brotherly kindness love" (A.S.V.). Faith is the foundation; love is the capstone, the greatest of the Christian graces (I Cor. 13:13).

Jude's admonition may therefore be understood quite literally. We bear the responsibility for self-development, for growth in Christian character, for the rearing of a structure that will glorify Christ in everything. The use of the present participle, *building,* indicates that this is to be a lifelong task.

How does one build up himself? The answer is found in Acts 20:32: "I commend you to God, and to the word of his grace, which is able to build you up." We build ourselves up by applying the teachings of the Scriptures to our lives. Faith comes by hearing the Word (Rom. 10:17). Cleansing from

sin is provided in the Word (Eph. 5:26; John 17:17).
Obedience to the Word brings blessing untold (James 1:25).
When we desire it, we grow thereby (I Peter 2:2). "Whoso
keepeth his word, in him verily is the love of God perfected"
(I John 2:5).

"Praying in the Holy Spirit" is a phrase which unites two
words each of which appears more than a hundred times in
the New Testament, the words for prayer and for the Spirit
of God. They are found together also in Ephesians 6:18:
"Praying always with all prayer and supplication in the
Spirit." Of six distinct words for prayer used in the New
Testament this is the most common. It refers to our regular
communion with God in which we make known our petitions
to Him. However, Paul's double use of the word "praying
. . . with all prayer" indicates that it may include all forms
of prayer and thanksgiving as well. Jude emphasizes the vital
life-breath of the Christian, his unending communion with
God, but doubtless he likewise has in view those deeper
strivings and beseechings which drive us to our knees in
times of great urgency.

Prayer in the Spirit is prayer which issues from a heart
indwelt, illuminated, and controlled by the Holy Spirit of
God. It is petition, praise, and thanksgiving which are indited
by the Spirit. The outstanding inspired commentary upon it
is found in Romans 8:26, 27. By ourselves, we know not
how to pray as we ought, but there dwells within us One who
makes intercession for us with unutterable groanings, intercession which is in accordance with the will of God.

"Keep yourselves in the love of God." Again we are looking at the other side of a truth of which the first side has
already appeared in our epistle. Verse 1 reveals that we are
"kept for Jesus Christ"; that is God's side. Here is our side.
Because we are "kept by the power of God" (I Peter 1:5),
we are to keep ourselves in the conscious enjoyment of
God's love.

This is in contrast with the other record given by Jude in
relation to this word *keep*. Fallen angels kept not their own

principality, and so they are kept in everlasting bonds under darkness unto the judgment of the great day. The implication is clear concerning the apostates described in this epistle. They once tasted the good Word of God, which reveals the love of God, but they did not drink in that Word. They never permitted themselves to know God's love experimentally. Therefore, they are more fittingly pictured by the angels who are kept for judgment than the saints who are kept for Jesus Christ.

We are not to understand this admonition as though it read, "Keep on loving God." Not our love for Him, but His love for us is in view. The passage is similar to John 15:9: "As the Father hath loved me, so have I loved you: continue ye in my love." We bear the responsibility in both passages for keeping ourselves, or continuing, in the sphere within which the love of God is able to bless us.

The prodigal of Luke 15 was still beloved by his father when he went away to a far country, but he had removed himself from the place where he could enjoy the benefits of his father's love to the fullest. He did not keep himself in the love of his father.

How are we to obey this precept? The answer is given in John 15:10: "If ye keep my commandments, ye shall abide in my love." To abide is to continue or to keep oneself in the sunshine of His love. We abide when we obey the Word of God (cf. I John 3:23).

A look ahead for the Christian concludes Jude's fourfold rule. We are to be "looking for the mercy of our Lord Jesus Christ unto eternal life." The Greek word translated "looking for" is given the sense of "waiting for" in four passages, of which Luke 12:36 is representative. We are to be "like unto men that wait for their Lord." In four passages also it is rendered as in the passage before us, of which Titus 2:13 is closest to Jude 21: "Looking for that blessed hope, and the glorious appearing of the great God and our Saviour Jesus Christ."

We are to be living in an atmosphere of eager anticipation

of the coming of our Lord. When He comes, there will be judgment on the adversaries, but mercy for us. While we wait and look, we know that we have eternal life, but we know there is more to come, in the redemption of our bodies and the experience of the fullness of the meaning of that wonderful reality, eternal life. Mercy is multiplied unto us now (Jude 2), but it will not have its consummation until He comes again "the second time without sin unto salvation" (Heb. 9:28).

These wonderful verses begin with an inward look at the developing of Christian character; we are to be building. They continue with an outward look at everything and everyone for whom we should intercede; we are to be praying. Then they look upward at the One who loves us and who has made us His children; we are to keep ourselves in the love of God. They conclude with a forward look at the return of our Saviour and the dawn of eternal life in His presence; we are to be looking and waiting for the final great manifestation of His mercy.

There is progress of doctrine here, from faith through love to the blessed hope. There is work and prayer and service and anticipation. The three Persons of the Trinity are set forth, the Holy Spirit, God the Father, and the Lord Jesus Christ. Any one of these themes would greatly enrich the mind and deepen the experience of the believer who traced it throughout the Scriptures. Brief though these verses are, they would repay careful study and quiet meditation.

WINNING THE LOST

And on some have mercy, who are in doubt; and some save, snatching them out of the fire; and on some have mercy with fear; hating even the garment spotted by the flesh (vv. 22, 23).

THE LAST MESSAGE of Jude before his closing benediction is a revelation of the sacred duty of believers toward those who have not yet been born again. This ought not to surprise us, because God is compassionate, no matter how terrible His judgments, or how dreadful the doom He has decreed for those who deny our only Master and Lord Jesus Christ. God loves those who are enticed by the men of whom this epistle speaks. He has commissioned all who know the truth to seek and to save the lost by presenting to them the good news of free salvation.

No sooner have we finished reading what we are to do for ourselves in the presence of ungodly mockers, when we discover that these truths do not stand alone. They are inseparable from the truth of what we are to do for others. There is no interruption in the flow of thought between verses 21 and 23. We cannot escape these instructions concerning personal witness. It is a wonderful thing to see how the last admonition of Jude, like the last words of the Lord whom he served, have to do with soul-winning (Luke 24:46-49).

In a brief manual for personal work three groups of people are set before us: (1) those who need compassionate tenderness, because sincere doubts trouble them; (2) those requiring urgent boldness if they are to be snatched from an eternity of fiery judgment; and (3) those who must be dealt with in cautious compassion lest the soul-winner himself be contaminated by their sins.

We are the recipients of great mercy. It is multiplied to us now (Jude 2); we look for an abundant manifestation of it in the future, at the return of our Saviour (v. 21). It is only fitting, therefore, that we should be merciful to others. We are surrounded by people who are in doubt. Unless we obey verse 22, their honest doubts will give way to eternal despair.

The very first use of this word *mercy* in the New Testament is in the promise: "Blessed are the merciful: for they shall obtain mercy" (Matt. 5:7). It is profitable to place this passage alongside the last use of the word in the Bible, which is in the portion now before us.

Who are the merciful of whom Christ spoke? Certainly they include those who have compassion on the lost and seek to win them to the Saviour. When do they obtain mercy? Although it is multiplied to them throughout life, it is received in greatest measure when all the fullness of eternal life dawns upon the soul at the second coming of Christ for His Church. Blessed indeed are all soul-winners. Blessed means happy, and no greater joy is found than the joy of extending mercy to the lost by bringing them to a personal experience of salvation.

The Gospel of Matthew also presents the first use of the word *doubt* found in Jude 22 (Matt. 14:31). The law of first mention states that the first occurrence of a word in the Scriptures often underlines something significant about its later usages. Matthew records how Peter heard the invitation of Christ to come to Him. He began to obey, but fear filled his heart, and he started to sink into the sea. When he cried, "Lord, save me!" immediately "Jesus stretched forth his hand, and caught him, and said unto him, O thou of little faith, wherefore didst thou doubt?"

Let us keep this record in mind as we study Jude. Despite Christ's invitation to come unto Him, many are fearful. Because they doubt His power to save, they are ready to sink into perdition. As His representatives, we are to reach out the hand of compassion to them, tell them all they need is a cry of helpless trust, "Lord, save me." When they call He hears them and saves them out of all their troubles (Ps. 34:6). Thus we obey the words, "and on some have mercy, who are in doubt."

Another rendering of this verse is given in the margin, "and some refute while they dispute with you." If this is to be accepted as a better translation of an admittedly difficult Greek text, it is well illustrated in verse 9 of our epistle. Michael contended with the Devil when he disputed over the body of Moses. A dispute is sometimes forced upon the soul-winner. Although it is true that argument is usually unwise in dealing with the lost, here is a passage requiring us to refute, or to convict, those who dispute with us.

To contend and lose is indeed a serious matter, but to contend and win is to win a soul forever. Therefore we are to be ready to give an answer for the hope that is within us (I Peter 3:15). We are to be prepared to demonstrate the falsity of an opponent's position, in the power and the wisdom of the Holy Spirit. Our own lack of wisdom in such a situation is the condition for securing the wisdom which God supplies (James 1:5).

The Spirit tells us to refute or convict those who oppose our witness. We can do this if we build ourselves up on our most holy faith, pray in the Spirit, keep ourselves in the love of God, and live as those who await their returning Lord. In our hands the Word can become the Sword of the Spirit to pierce the heart, a hammer to break down opposition. The word *refute* actually means more than to persuade successfully. It carries a punitive idea, as in Hebrews 12:5, where it is translated "rebuked" with reference to the chastisement of God. The Word of God can refute; it can punish; it can convict; it can convert. Every believer ought to have some personal experience of the meaning of this phrase of

Scripture. When the Lord comes, He will convict the ungodly of all their works of ungodliness (Jude 15). Before He
comes, we have the responsibility of convicting men of their
sin by His Word in the power of His Spirit. If we succeed,
they will escape the judgment foretold by Enoch. They may
choose between being convicted now, or being convicted
then. The difference is as great as the width of the chasm
dividing Heaven from Hell.

Another class of unsaved persons is to be saved by snatching them out of the fire. There is no reason to suppose that
Jude is referring to something other than the eternal fire
mentioned in verse 7. The law of first mention would lead
us to think this is true, because Matthew 3:10-12 speaks of
"unquenchable fire," and the law of last mention would con-
firm it—"the lake which burneth with fire and brimstone:
which is the second death" (Rev. 21:8).

Lot and his daughters were snatched as brands from the
burning (Gen. 19:15, 16, 24). They are the classic illustration of Jude 23, and the appropriateness of the illustration
is underscored by the fact that prayer in the Holy Spirit is
found in each context. Jude enjoins this upon us; Genesis
records the fact that the reason for the mercy of the Lord
being granted to Lot was the intercession of godly Abraham.
Only when such prayer is offered are men snatched from the
everlasting burnings (Isa. 33:14).

What these men have done, who are so close to Hell fire,
Jude does not inform us, but the story of Lot suggests that
they are living in close contact with fleshly sin. Is there something about such sin which tends to set a man apart from
the conviction of the Spirit in some degree, so that his danger
of perdition is the greater? We dare not say so, yet passages
like Mark 9:43-48 may imply something like this. Matthew
5:22 states that a man who calls his brother a fool is in
danger of Hell fire, while Matthew 23:33 raises the question
of how a hypocrite (Matt. 23:29) can escape the damnation
of Hell.

Two other Old Testament illustrations belong with our passage in Jude. Amos 4:11 refers to Israel as "a firebrand plucked out of the burning." Zechariah 3:1, 2 describes Joshua, the high priest of Israel, as standing before the angel of the Lord, with Satan standing at his right hand to resist him. "And the Lord said unto Satan, The Lord rebuke thee, O Satan; even the Lord that hath chosen Jerusalem rebuke thee; is not this a brand plucked out of the fire?"

Even the high priest of Israel was a man who had been snatched from the flames! This should encourage us to hope that some of those who now seem hopelessly lost in sin may become useful servants of Christ, if we heed the Scriptures and pluck them out. No case should be regarded as hopeless. The history of soul-winning is filled with the records of men and women so far gone in sin that it seemed as though the flames of Hell were about to receive them, when some messenger of the cross snatched them out of the fire, and they became outstanding evangelists and personal workers afterward.

The third class of sinners with whom we are told to deal are to be approached with fear. We are not told that they are in a worse condition than those who are to be snatched from the flames, but that we are in greater danger in dealing with them, even though they may not themselves be on the verge of perdition. We hardly would consider ourselves to be in danger of spiritual contamination in dealing with a poor drunkard on the verge of perdition, or the condemned inmate of some prison. Yet there are types of sin or of sinners which not only may be said to threaten the spiritual life of the soul-winner, but which have actually ensnared more than one servant of Christ. Most Christian leaders know of cases where a once useful follower of the Lord fell into grievous fleshly sin because he did not heed Jude's warning.

The warnings of the Book of Proverbs well illustrate this point of mingling our zeal with godly fear. The fear of the Lord is the beginning of knowledge and of wisdom, even in soul-winning (Prov. 1:7; 9:10). "A wise man feareth, and departeth from evil" (14:16). "Enter not into the path of the wicked, and go not in the way of evil men. Avoid it, pass not by it, turn from it, and pass away" (4:14, 15).

Some have thought they could better win the socially prominent by taking a social glass with them, only to become enslaved by wine. Yet the Word says: "Look not thou upon the wine when it is red" (Prov. 23:31). Others have lost their usefulness through covetousness, during a ministry among the very wealthy, but Proverbs 23:4 warns: "Labor not to be rich: cease from thine own wisdom."

There is for some a temptation to try to win those who oppose the truth by toning down the Gospel, or compromising with unbelief. This danger would be avoided if Proverbs 19:27 were heeded: "Cease, my son, to hear the instruction that causeth to err from the words of knowledge"; or Proverbs 28:4: "They that forsake the law praise the wicked: but such as keep the law contend with them."

The commonest illustration of failure to listen to Jude's admonition to have mercy with fear is found in ministry to members of the opposite sex. One of the basic rules of successful soul-winners is that it is wise to deal with one's own sex. The man who ignores this precept, who forgets the many faithful warnings of Proverbs (6:23, ff.; 7:25; 9:16), who overlooks the last principle of witness set forth by Jude, does so at his peril. The fear of the Lord delivers from such dangers (Prov. 2:5, 16).

"Hating even the garment spotted by the flesh." What is the meaning of this phrase? Difficulties in the Greek text make dogmatism impossible, but there is a striking parallel between Jude 22, 23 and Zechariah 3:1-5 which seems to point to a good answer. Using the marginal rendering supplied in the American Standard Version (1901), we find three things listed in order by Jude: the refutation of disputers, the snatching of men from the fire, and mercy to those who are clothed with filthy garments. These same three things appear also in Zechariah. Satan is rebuked for disputing or resisting the salvation of Joshua; Joshua is called "a brand plucked out of the fire"; Joshua is seen clothed in filthy garments which are taken from him.

We may therefore suggest that Zechariah throws light upon Jude by placing a threefold illustration before the soul-winner. Those who dispute with us are actually tools of Satan, who must be rebuked in the name of the Lord if we are to win them (I Peter 5:8, 9). Again, those whom we pluck from the fire are individuals in whom the Lord has a personal interest, and we may count upon His help in our superhuman task. He stands with us; His Word directs us; His love encompasses even those whose sin is like an evil contagion. Finally, those whom Jude here describes must be seen as God sees them, as clothed in filthy garments. There may be a superficial, or even a very real attractiveness about some forms of sin, else we would not be warned concerning some types of sinners. But beyond the surface, within the aura of glamor, gaiety, and seductive appearance lurks the filthy garment of soul-destroying sin. A desirable Babylonish garment, a bag of silver, and a wedge of gold attracted and destroyed Achan (Josh. 7). We must hate the garment, the silver, and the gold of sin. We must see that the filthy robes are given up for the raiment of salvation (Isa. 61:10), without permitting ourselves to entertain a secret longing for that which God warns us against (II Tim. 4:10).

It is customary simply to regard this difficult passage as a proverbial expression. We are to have mercy, while hating everything having to do with the sin of the men to whom we bear witness, even down to their *kiton*, or inner robe, which is a symbol of all that touches or surrounds the sinner. As the garment is spotted by the flesh, so the atmosphere in which some live is defiled, and capable of defiling the child of God. He must hate the atmosphere, the environment, the alluring garments in which sin is sometimes arrayed.

If we exhibit true godly fear in dealing with persons whose

sin could contaminate us, we shall shun their form of sin as we would avoid the plague. We shall "avoid it, pass not by it, turn from it," lest we find ourselves infected. We shall be as careful as Israel was commanded to be in the presence of leprosy or other communicable diseases (Lev. 13:45-47). Yet we shall be as merciful and compassionate as we can be, in view of what the Scriptures command, and what the Spirit enables us to do.

THE GRAND BENEDICTION

Now unto him that is able to guard you from stumbling,
and to set you before the presence of his glory without
blemish in exceeding joy, to the only God our Saviour,
through Jesus Christ our Lord, be glory, majesty, dominion
and power, before all time, and now, and forevermore. Amen
(vv. 24, 25).

As THE EPISTLE BEGAN, so it ends, with words of assurance for God's people living in dark days. Will they be able to keep themselves in the love of God? Can they avoid contamination in their contacts with the ungodly? Is it possible for them always to walk uprightly in the land of the living? The answer is made crystal clear. They can so live, because the One who loved them and gave Himself for them is able also to keep them from falling.

In all of the broad sweep of truth concerning apostasy found in our study, there is nothing to suggest that a true child of God can become an apostate. Nevertheless, the fear of this can creep into the hearts of some who are aware of an evil tendency toward unbelief within themselves. For the comfort of such, and for the instruction of us all, the Lord has caused it to be written that He is able to guard us even from stumbling.

Long before these words were penned, the practical secret of how a believer can lay hold of this divine ability to keep us from tripping and falling was written in Proverbs 3:19-23. When it is our life purpose to seek the wisdom of God, and to be guided by the understanding and knowledge of God made available to us in His Word, we have the ancient promise: "Then shalt thou walk in thy way safely, and thy foot shall not stumble." Here is the secret of how Enoch and Noah both walked with God. This truth is basic to the more than thirty New Testament admonitions regarding our walk as Christians (I Thess. 4:1).

But there is another figure in the Scriptures. Not only are we called upon to walk; we must also "run with patience the race that is set before us" (Heb. 12:1). Again we find in the Book of Proverbs instructions telling us how we can run our race without stumbling. "Hear, O my son, and receive my sayings. . . . When thou runnest, thou shalt not stumble" (Prov. 4:10, 12). The lesson is essentially the same one. Respect for what the Bible teaches is the secret. The full teaching is so far beyond the mere avoidance of stumbling that we read of those who wait upon the Lord: "They shall run, and not be weary; and they shall walk, and not faint" (Isa. 40:31).

If a Christian does stumble, it is not because God has failed him. The Lord is able and willing to keep us upright as we travel in paths of righteousness. As we honor the Word, meditating therein day and night, it becomes a staff in our hand. It becomes the means whereby God is able to preserve our steps.

An apostate despises the Word, stumbles and falls. When a true child of God turns away from the means of grace and stumbles, the Scripture is fulfilled which reads: "Though he fall, he shall not be utterly cast down: for the Lord upholdeth him with his hand" (Ps. 37:24). Just as an earthly father delights in the steps of his small child as he ventures to walk with his hand in his, so our heavenly Father watches over us. He is interested in our progress. He will not allow us to destroy ourselves. He is indeed able to guard us from stumbling. If we take our hand from His, and a rough place in the road trips us up, He is able to put us back on our feet. "He restoreth my soul," wrote the psalmist, drawing upon the experience of the shepherd who brings a poor straying sheep back into the path from which it has wandered.

Now comes a sudden transition. He is able "to set you before the presence of his glory." Jude overleaps all the vicissitudes of life, all the grievous experiences of Christians who do not take full advantage of the strength and power God has made available to preserve them. He speaks of their being set at last before the presence of the One who died for them. This is the highest pinnacle of truth in the entire epistle. Already Jude has revealed that we are kept for Jesus Christ. He has spoken of the Lord's coming to earth in judgment, accompanied by His holy ones. But now he describes in one breathtaking utterance that moment of rapturous fulfillment of the hope of the ages when we shall see our Lord in His glory.

From the possibility of present stumbling we are suddenly translated to Christ in the glory. Surely there is meaning in this divinely chosen order of words. Does it not suggest that in such an hour as we think not, the Lord shall come for us? Is not the rapture of the Church in view? One moment we are concerned with our earthly pilgrimage and the rough road we often find ourselves traveling. In the next moment that is all in the past, and we are with our blessed Lord, surrounded by glory. This is enough to encourage the most sorely tried pilgrim with the hope that beyond the next faltering step may lie his eternal home in the skies. Now he is walking step by step, in utter dependence on his God. All at once, like Enoch, he finds the God he loved and served intervening to translate him, to take him away without dying. No wonder this is called the blessed hope.

When God our Saviour picks us up from our walk upon earth and sets us before the presence of His glory, we are to be "without blemish." He is able to do this, writes Jude, and he is almost echoing the words of the apostle Paul. When Christ loved the Church and gave Himself for it, it was so that "he might sanctify and cleanse it with the wash-

ing of water by the word, That he might present it to himself a glorious church, not having spot, or wrinkle, or any
such thing; but that it should be holy and without blemish"
(Eph. 5:26, 27). Paul is speaking of cleansing and wash-
ing, just as Jude is speaking of stumbling, when he also by a
sudden transition describes the Church as presented in glory
before the presence of her Saviour and Lord.

Both passages describe the moment of fulfillment of
Christ's words in John 17:24: "Father, I will that they also,
whom thou hast given me, be with me where I am; that they
may behold my glory, which thou hast given me." In that
wonderful moment, for which both Paul and Jude use the
same Greek word *amomos,* without blemish, to describe our
condition, we shall be conformed to the image of the Son
of God, because the very same word is used of Him in
I Peter 1:19, "a lamb without blemish and without spot." "We
shall be like him; for we shall see him as he is" (I John
3:2).

At that time, when the blemishes of this life are gone forever, our state is further described as one of "exceeding
joy." This is the same Greek root rendered "greatly rejoice" in Peter's description of those who contemplate entering into their inheritance (I Peter 1:6). It appears also in
that remarkable statement of the believer's anticipation of
beholding the Person of Christ at His return (I Peter 1:8),
where it becomes "joy unspeakable and full of glory." Its
final occurrence is in the overwhelming passage devoted to
the alleluias of the saints in glory, ending with the voice of
the great multitude: "Alleluia: for the Lord God omnip-
otent reigneth. Let us be glad and rejoice, and give honor
to him: for the marriage of the Lamb is come" (Rev. 19:6,
7).

Unto the only God our Saviour, Jude now ascribes glory,
majesty, dominion and power forever, and closes his epistle
with an Amen. Why does he speak of "God our Saviour
through Jesus Christ our Lord"? It may be suggested that

it is to emphasize for one last time the great truth denied by apostasy, the fact that God is Saviour only for those who come to Him through Jesus Christ. No man cometh to the Father but by the Son. Those who think that believing in God is equivalent to being eternally saved, without reference to the cross of Christ, cannot put down the Epistle of Jude without a final reminder that the Word of God contradicts their position. God is Saviour only through Christ. Millions may express belief in one God, may offer a form of worship, without being able to claim Him as Saviour because they deny His Son. "For there is one God, and one mediator between God and men, the man Christ Jesus" (I Tim. 2:5).

Only the God of Jude, the God of evangelical Christianity, may properly be called "God our Saviour," because only those who accept the truth of Jude 25, John 14:6, and Acts 4:12 acknowledge that salvation is through the Lord Jesus Christ alone.

The Bible-believing Christian is not at all surprised at Jude's calling God Saviour, while clearly distinguishing Him from His Son, because this same expression is used elsewhere in the New Testament (I Tim. 1:1; 2:3; Titus 3:4-6). In the last of these passages is found the amazing double reference—"the kindness and love of God our Saviour toward man . . . through Jesus Christ our Saviour." Passages in the Old Testament like Psalm 106:21 and Isaiah 60:16 use similar terminology, while Psalm 80:1-3 presents the remarkable truth that the God who should one day come and save His people is also the Shepherd.

Human language cannot contain the fullness of the meaning of the four words used by Jude to ascribe praise and worship to God in his grand benediction. What are glory, majesty, dominion, and power? Perhaps the closest we can approach to a comprehension of this fourfold reference to some of the attributes of God is to take our cue from Hebrews 1:3, where all four are associated in the only other New Testament passage including them all.

Glory is the brightness, the manifested excellence of God. It is a divine radiance which shines (Luke 2:9); which blinds (Acts 22:11); which cannot be endured by the unglorified human race, and which therefore is protected by the smoke of the divine Presence (Rev. 15:8).

Majesty, a word found only here and in Hebrews 1:3 and 8:1, refers to the incomparable, ineffable regal presence of the Ruler of the universe. It suggests the omniscience of God upon His throne.

Dominion may be said to contemplate the infinite extent of the strong rule of God throughout His universe. He upholdeth "all things by the word of his power" (Heb. 1:3); "his kingdom ruleth over all" (Ps. 103:19). Dominion suggests the omnipresence of the glorious Majesty on high.

Power is the irresistible divine authority and might exercised by our God. It suggests His omnipotence.

And yet when we have tried our best to say something about Jude's four words, we must admit our failure adequately to define or explain them, and rest upon that inexplicable God-given ability to grasp their meaning in spite of the poverty of human language, that ability which is the portion of every true child of God as he sings the Alleluia Chorus, or reads such an ascription of praise to God as David's: "Thine, O Lord, is the greatness, and the power, and the glory, and the victory, and the majesty: for all that is in the heaven and in the earth is thine; thine is the kingdom, O Lord, and thou art exalted as head above all" (I Chron. 29:11).

Having comprehended the glorious brightness, the unutterable regal Being of the One who sits upon the throne, the limitless extent of His rule, and the unlimited strength of His might, Jude can write no more. He tries to encompass eternity within the poor limits of human vocabulary, and in so doing supplies us with one of the most remarkable utterances ever penned upon such a subject, then closes his inspired epistle.

"Before all time, and now, and forevermore." What a way to end a letter! Before the stars were set in their courses to mark off time, throughout all the ages which have been recorded in Heaven since time began, and on into the measureless future of God's unfolding purposes, these four divine attributes have belonged, do now belong, and will forever belong to God. In the wonder of the contemplation of such truths, the pen of the inspired apostle is laid down, his lips become dumb.

All Jude can do is say, "Amen," which is to say, "Verily! What I have written is true; these are faithful words." And every true believer will echo the last word of the last epistle of the New Testament, supporting his Amen with actions and attitudes suited to the solemn revelations which God has been pleased to set forth to warn and instruct us in the dark days which are ahead before the great apostasy has run its final course.

THE END